T0114355

A WOMAN CLOTHED

WITH THE SUN

A WOMAN CLOTHED

WITH THE SUN

EIGHT GREAT APPEARANCES

OF OUR LADY IN

MODERN TIMES

JOHN J. DELANEY, EDITOR

IMAGE BOOKS | DOUBLEDAY

New York London Toronto Sydney Auckland

AN IMAGE BOOK
PUBLISHED BY DOUBLEDAY
a division of Random House, Inc.
1540 Broadway, New York, New York 10036

IMAGE, DOUBLEDAY, and the portrayal of a deer drinking from
a stream are trademarks of Doubleday, a division of Random
House, Inc.

First Image edition published September 1961
by special arrangement with Doubleday.
This Image edition published April 2001.

NIHIL OBITAT: ✠ James F. Rigney, S.T.D.
                    Censor Librorum

IMPRIMATUR: Francis Cardinal Spellman
                  Archbishop of New York
                  November 4, 1959

The selections on pages 167 to 168 from *Our Lady of
Fatima*, copyright 1947 by William Thomas Walsh,
are used by permission of The Macmillan Company.

The Library of Congress has cataloged the 1961 Image
edition as follows:
A Woman Clothed with the Sun: eight great
appearances of Our Lady in modern times.
John J. Delaney, editor.
     p.   cm.
Reprint. Originally published: New York:
Hanover House, 1960
1. Mary, Blessed Virgin, Saint—Apparitions
and miracles. I. Delaney, John J.
BT650.W65 1990   89-29888
232.91'7—dc20   CIP

ISBN 0-385-08019-0

Book design by Pei Loi Koay

147429898

TO ANN

most loving and faithful of wives;

most constant of companions;

most understanding of friends;

my beloved.

CONTENTS

OUR LADY'S
APPARITIONS

John J. Delaney

During the past few decades there has been a steady and ever-growing stream of books on Our Lady. Her life on earth, her position in Catholic teaching, her relationship to mankind and her significance to man's salvation, the increasing attention to the concept of her as Mediatrix of all Graces, her role as the Mother of God—all these and other innumerable aspects of her life, personality, and role have been considered and analyzed in recent years.

Despite this great outpouring, it is clearly evident that the inspiration for these books provides a rich and inexhaustible source for further study and benefit to mankind. The more men study Our Lady, the more they unearth new and exciting aspects of her life, significance, and influence that have great importance in today's world. Here is a subject that is ever new, fraught with the utmost importance and deeply meaningful in a world in which she is so clearly evincing deep interest and grave concern.

One of the most significant aspects of modern life has been the repeated visitations of Our Lady from her heavenly home to earth. Especially in the last century Our Lady has become more and more concerned with the affairs of man. Repeatedly, she has intervened to warn men that they are treading on the brink of destruction, and to point out the way to salvation. So prominent a feature of Catholic life have these apparitions become that the expression "Marian Age" is often assigned to our times.

In view of the importance of these interventions in human affairs, it occurred to me that it would be most useful to select a group of the outstanding apparitions of Our Lady and tell the story of these appearances in a simple, straightforward manner. With the exceptions of Banneux and Beauraing, each of these apparitions has been widely written about in the English-speaking world. As the deeper implications of these visits have been realized there has been a tendency to concentrate on their profound theological significance and meaning. Books of this nature are of the utmost importance. It is only by such discussion and consideration that fundamental doctrines are refined and applied within the body of Catholic dogma. But, at the same time, there is a definite place for a concise, lucid presentation of these appearances which can be read for a better understanding of Our Lady's messages by the average reader who does not have the scholarly background necessary to read and understand the more learned studies of these visits.

With this thought in mind, I approached a group of distinguished authorities on Our Lady and asked each one to write on the particular apparition of Our Lady with which he or she has been closely connected. In many cases the person selected is regarded as *the* outstanding authority on the apparition about which he or she writes; in every case there is unquestioned competence and ability to write of the apparition considered.

In each article the contributor tells straightforwardly and simply the story of the apparition, including: the background for the visitation, local and world-wide; descriptions of the persons who saw Our Lady, their family background, education, and faith; a description of the actual apparition; how the announcement of the vision was received; and, finally, the message for the world and the significance to mankind of each particular vision. The result is a thorough treatment of each apparition which tells with new freshness the awe-inspiring stories of the visits of the Mother of God to her children on earth.

A word should be said about the selection of apparitions to be included in this book. No attempt has been made to present a complete collection of every appearance of Our Lady. Obviously, then, to some extent, those included must be an arbitrary selection of the editor.

In making such an arbitrary selection an editor inevitably will be chided for not including this apparition or that vision. I must admit that the selection of these eight apparitions is arbitrary in the sense that they are the visions that the editor has selected to present. Unquestionably, there are other authentic apparitions which might well have been included. Nevertheless, to my own mind, the eight appearances of Our Lady here considered are the outstanding apparitions of Our Lady in modern times and contain the essential elements of all of the apparitions of Our Lady. Nevertheless, it might be worth while to pause a moment and discuss them briefly.

Obviously, La Salette, Lourdes, and Fatima do not have to be defended on any grounds. Few authorities would refuse them a place among the greatest apparitions of Our Lady. Their effect on Catholics and, indeed, on all mankind is yet to be realized. Any book of apparitions which does not contain these three must perforce be a travesty.

Guadalupe is included although it is earlier than the other seven (which took place in the slightly over hundred-year span from 1830 to 1933) because it has a particular importance which is becoming apparent today. It happened in a new country (after all Columbus had only discovered America in 1492) sparsely settled, largely unexplored, and inhabited by savages. At first blush it might seem a rather peculiar place for Our Lady to appear. Nevertheless, it seems to me there are two tremendously important reasons for this apparition. As I will point out later, one of the significant features of all of the apparitions here considered is the youth of Our Lady. America, at that time, was to most men the newest section of the world. It offered to all mankind the fulfillment of dreams of wealth, honor, and adventure. Here among the nations of the world was a fresh, youthful paradise offering new hope and promising untold benefits to all men from the most exalted to the humblest. Just as she, in her youth, is an ever-new, ever-fresh source of hope and inspiration for mankind, so in the centuries ahead America was to be the hope of countless millions, the refuge of the poor, the homeless, and the oppressed.

I would like to think that Our Lady deliberately chose America for this appearance to emphasize that this was to be a land of more than mere material wealth and personal advantage—that rather, here was a land which would make a spiritual contribution to the world's welfare beyond the wildest dreams of its inhabitants and conquerors. It seems to me that Our Lady was indicating four centuries ago that this was a land on which she smiled and that here was a land from which, in the future, the Church would be able to draw great strength and sustenance. What has happened in the United States in the past half century amply justifies this point. During that period the Church in the United States has developed one of the strongest, wealthiest, and most active groups of Catholics in the world. Time and again the Holy See—and, indeed, the whole world—has turned to America for material aid and America has responded nobly. Now, in addition to material resources, America, for the first time in her history, is in a position to repay some of the spiritual indebtedness she has incurred. American missionaries are going abroad to help win new lands and converts for the Church; American prelates are assuming positions of great importance in Church affairs; American scholars, writers, artists are beginning to contribute to our Catholic culture; Americans are making real beginnings in the sphere of religion, as witness the increase of contemplative foundations in the United States. These are just a few indications of the trend in the development of American Catholicism. All this, it seems clear, was portended by Our Lady in Guadalupe. It is no mere coincidence that the United States has as its patron the Immaculate Conception. Considered in this light, Guadalupe must be included in any important collection of Our Lady's apparitions.

Considering the incredible spread in the devotion to the Miraculous Medal in the last century, certainly no defense or justification for including this apparition is needed. When Our Lady appeared to St. Catherine Labouré in 1830, she, as Father Dirvin puts it in his article, "heralded a new Marian day, a day of such duration that it would be called the Age of Mary." What more need be said?

Beauraing and Banneux have been included because there are several unusual aspects of these apparitions which seem to demand their inclusion among the most important apparitions. They occurred within the lifetime of most people living today. The scorn and skepticism with which they were greeted, particularly in the case of Banneux, reflects perfectly the modern tone of skepticism and derision toward all matters concerning faith. That despite this reception both Beauraing and Banneux, after intensive ecclesiastical investigation, were accepted as authentic seems to me a portent of how faith will eventually conquer the "rationalistic" philosophies which held sway for so long over men's minds. Could it be that the Age of Enlightenment is about to succumb to the Age of Mary?

And, finally, Knock is included because it so clearly foreshadowed the tremendous resurgence of interest in the liturgy, particularly of the Mass, which has grown by leaps and bounds in the past decade. This is the only apparition of Our Lady so closely associated with the celebration of the Mass though other apparitions clearly indicated her interest, as for instance in Fatima where, as a prelude to the actual apparitions, an angel administered Communion to the children. She so clearly indicated that she wanted closer participation in the Mass that it is almost unbelievable it has taken a century for the message to sink in.

These, briefly, are the reasons why these particular apparitions have been selected for inclusion. I readily concede that other apparitions might well be added. Nevertheless, these eight apparitions, in their variety and comprehensiveness, are representative of all of Our Lady's appearances. Most important of all, they contain all of the basic ingredients of the over-all message which she is striving so desperately to give the human race.

A word about the attitude of the Church regarding apparitions and miracles. As is true of all the Church's pronouncements, her teaching on this matter is logical, and yet at the same time it allows the greatest possible personal freedom to the individual. According to this teaching, a miracle is an unusual event performed by God or through His intervention which cannot be explained by the ordinary laws of nature. The Church demands that her children accept as a matter of faith the principle that miracles occur.

Also as a matter of faith Catholics must specifically believe in the miracles described in the Bible. Since the Bible is divinely inspired the miracles described therein must be accepted, since their validity is attested by the indisputable word of God; and the Bible is replete with incidents which can be described only as miracles and which can be accounted for only by the fact of supernatural intervention.

While on earth Our Lord Himself performed a variety of miracles: the raising of the dead; making the blind to see; curing lepers; making the deaf to hear; and of course the greatest of all miracles, His Resurrection from the dead. It would be ridiculous for the Church to teach anything but that these unusual occurrences were of supernatural origin—miracles—and that Catholics must believe them, since Our Lord performed them.

However, after her stricture that Catholics must believe that miracles can occur and must specifically accept those described in the Bible, the Church then allows the widest latitude for personal belief or unbelief in apparitions or miracles which have occurred since Biblical times.

"Apparition" is the name assigned to certain kinds of supernatural visions, either bodily or visible, and is the term most frequently applied to the various visions of Our Lady. The teaching of the Church regarding apparitions is comparable to her teaching about miracles which frequently stem from these apparitions. Briefly it is this.

Revelation as a source of knowledge and information about faith and morals is a true and infallible guidance for man and is to be found in the Bible. But public revelation ceased with the death of the last apostle. Everything necessary for man's salvation is found in the public deposit of faith which has been confided to the Church, *and to the Church only.* The Catholic Church was founded by Our Lord purposely to preserve and interpret His teaching in matters of faith and morals. Consequently, only the Church's teaching and authority bind us in these fields. Since the Church alone possesses this infallible *magisterium*, it necessarily follows that private revelations are not a part of Catholic faith and must be interpreted only according to the official teaching of the Church. Adolphe Tanquerey explains this clearly, in his *Spiritual Life*, when he says: "The assent to be given them is not, therefore, an act of Catholic faith, but one of human faith, based upon the fact that these revelations are probable and worthy of credence."

In short, an individual is free to reject any private revelation of modern times; but he is equally as free to accept any or all such private revelations as he desires—always, of course, with the knowledge that their interpretation is according to official Church teaching. Consequently, nobody is bound, as a matter of dogma, to believe that Our

Lady appeared at Fatima, or Lourdes, or La Salette, or any of the other places where she has been reported to have appeared at various times.

Nevertheless, when one considers the intensive ecclesiastical investigations to which these apparitions were subjected, and when one considers the unreserved judgment by proper ecclesiastical authorities that each of these apparitions is valid and worthy of having a cult established in its name, then rash indeed would be the individual who would question them. With the exception of Knock, every apparition described in this book has received appropriate and official episcopal approval. And even in the case of Knock intensive investigation has never caused a single witness to retract his or her testimony, and the Archbishop of Tuam, in whose archdiocese the apparition occurred, has for years joined in the processions and ceremonies which have grown up around the church in Knock. In all of the apparitions, churchmen of all rank, from humble clerics to cardinals, have freely testified to their belief in the authenticity of these apparitions and have participated in ceremonies at their sites frequently and in great numbers. Certainly the weight of evidence, from the Church's viewpoint, is so overwhelming in favor of these apparitions that it would be imprudent, to say the least, for any good Catholic to be skeptical of what the Church has so freely certified.

Before beginning the actual stories of the various apparitions it might be worth while to consider briefly some of the features common to all the appearances. Theologians are definitely convinced that there is a unified theme running through all of them. Obviously, the Mother of God does not appear capriciously and indiscriminately to individuals in isolated and unrelated sections of the world just to satisfy a whim. There is a definite purpose in every one of the appearances; there is a definite meaning to every aspect of each appearance; and, finally, there is a common message running through all of the apparitions that it behooves us to heed.

A consideration of some of these factors revealed in common in all of the appearances will be of great assistance in realizing that each of these appearances is related to each and all of the others. When these almost identical points are studied, our knowledge of the underlying and unifying message of all the apparitions becomes clearer in the light of their common relationship.

In considering some of the significant aspects of these eight apparitions which are common to all of the apparitions, I should make clear that it is not my intention to attempt to develop all of the theological implications of the various actions of Our Lady in these apparitions nor to consider every act or factor held in common in all the apparitions. Rather, what I would like to do is to present certain outstanding points which I feel in their own way are worth our consideration and which, considered as a group, contribute to the unity of the apparitions.

Among the points to be discussed are: the places Our Lady appeared; conditions in the area and the world at the time of the appearances; the persons to whom she appeared; her physical appearance; the phenomena accompanying her appearance; and, finally, the message which she left and which is constantly reiterated through all of her appearances. The treatment will necessarily be brief; but a résumé of these various points and their relationship should be most helpful in understanding the over-all relationship between the individual appearances.

A quick glance at the places Our Lady appeared reveals two interesting facts: first, with the exception of the Miraculous Medal apparition, they are in isolated, inaccessible areas; and second, religion in these areas was ignored, laughed at, or fiercely attacked. Even today, with our vaunted means of transportation, many of these places are still inaccessible. Mountainous regions and small, remote villages mainly in poverty-stricken communities and in places which seemed, as Monsignor Kennedy remarked in his book, *Light on the Mountain*, to be uniformly "Godforsaken places" are the rule. She did not appear in the beautiful gardens of Versailles, she did not appear in the lush vineyards of France, she did not appear in the rich wheat-growing areas of the Middle West in the United States, she did not appear in the castles of the rich or the universities of the learned. Rather, she appeared in barren areas which produced a livelihood for their inhabitants only after intensive cultivation and even then reluctantly. It almost seems that she was saying that it was not the areas fertile in the world's goods and knowledge that produced great faith in God but rather, as was the case of the desert fathers of ancient times and the monks of the early Christian era who built their monasteries in high mountainous areas, that she was emphasizing to mankind that things of the soul do not need things of the world to achieve spiritual fulfillment.

By the same token, the intellectual atmosphere in all the places that she appeared in these apparitions resembled closely the physical aspects of the areas. Skepticism, disbelief, ridicule, blasphemy, all of these were typical of the atmosphere of the places and the times in which she appeared. The "rationalism" of the nineteenth century was in full sway during the period covered by all of these apparitions, except Guadalupe, and even here, the opening of the New World was the beginning of the modern era which was to produce the flood of evils with which we are still contending. Faith was something to be scorned. Like Thomas, the individuals who controlled the society of the time would believe only if they were shown. Scientific method was in the ascendancy, progress was the word of the day, and the material betterment of mankind was the only goal worth seeking. Onto this scene like a bolt from heaven came the beautiful Lady, ignoring the barrenness of mind and country to reassert the beauty of faith and the love of God, without which mankind cannot exist.

As a corollary of these two facts is the interesting point that in all of these apparitions the countries where Our Lady appeared were Catholic. France, Belgium, Portugal, Ireland, through the centuries have been noted for the warm fervor of their Catholicism. At the time they were (and still are) regarded as Catholic countries, but in many of them unbelievers had gained control of the government and brainwashed much of the populace. It was almost as if Our Lady were calling men back to their ancient faith and rallying them against these forces which had taken over her beloved countries and peoples. Even Mexico, although a new country, was under the control of Spain, an ancient defender of the faith, and through the arduous labors of devoted and unselfish missionaries was even that early in her history turning to the Church. Here, again, it almost seemed as if Our Lady wanted to make certain that the people of this area, newly opened to the world's exploitation, would become her children.

Important as are the localities where Our Lady appeared, of far greater significance are the people to whom she appeared. With the exception of Juan Diego at Guadalupe, St. Catherine Labouré at the Miraculous Medal appearance, and the people at Knock, all of the visionaries were children. In the case of Juan Diego, his simplicity and naïveté would justify including him among the childlike visionaries; St. Catherine Labouré's complete and absolute devotion likewise would warrant including her in the category of child visionaries. Only in the case of Knock, which has several other unique features, were many of the spectators adult. Even here, though, the people involved were simple, devout, and childlike in the practice of their faith. In this connection it should be pointed out, too, that only at Knock did large numbers of people see the apparition.

All of the people who saw these apparitions, whether children or adults, had a common bond in their simplicity and innocence, almost as if Our Lady wanted a clean slate on which to write her message. In every instance, they were uneducated; even St. Catherine Labouré, strangely enough in view of her parents' background, had only a few months of formal schooling. It is evident that this was more than mere coincidence. When one considers the deep theological and philosophical amplifications of her messages and when one considers how anxious Mary was to have the word spread far and wide, the question naturally arises as to why she did not appear to learned scholars, people in important positions, or the great of the world. Certainly there were thousands of people in the various countries in which Our Lady appeared who were better able to understand and spread Our Lady's message and her instructions about building chapels or spreading devotions than were ignorant, unlettered Mariette Beco at Banneux or Catherine Labouré in the obscurity of her convent.

But it was not to the wealthy, to the influential, to the learned that Our Lady appeared. Rather it was to the poorest, humblest, most unlearned and illiterate of her children. And how right she was. These were people whose minds were uncluttered with the pretentious philosophies and skepticisms of the day or whose outlook on life was not befuddled by the complexities of the great savants' knowledge and teaching. These were the little people who would accept the fact that the Mother of God had appeared to them, unhesitatingly and unquestioningly. Directly and unequivocally, they would deliver the message she had given them exactly as she had given it to them, and no amount of questioning and bullying would change their stories. Their minds were so simple they were incapable of subterfuge, and in every case, prolonged investigation only strengthened their stories in the minds of fair-minded investigators.

When one pauses to relate Our Lady's appearances to the facts of her life on earth with her Blessed Son, the selection of the places and persons to whom she appeared becomes even more significant. Need the reader be reminded that Our Lord was born in a stable in Bethlehem; that He was raised the son of a poor carpenter; and that the main part of His preaching was to the common people? One need look no further than the Twelve He selected to spread the word of His Church to realize how closely Our Lady was following in His footsteps in the background and character of the people to whom she appeared.

There is a tremendous lesson to be learned here if we will but listen. It would seem she was saying clearly to man that he must approach knowledge and learning with the greatest of caution. Man has always been tempted to be vainglorious about his intellectual achievements, particularly in the modern era when our knowledge of the earth and the universe has been so tremendously increased. Wise men know that this knowledge so laboriously and painstakingly built up over the centuries is infinitesimal when compared to the only complete knowledge—that of God who *created* the universe whose secrets man is probing. But man, intoxicated with knowledge, tends to ascribe to his own intellect far more than it can ever attain.

By the nature of her appearances and those she selected to see her, Our Lady emphasized the fact that far more important than knowledge and learning is an uncomplicated faith which believes. How reminiscent of the words of Our Lord, "Blessed are they that have not seen, and have believed" (John 20:29). When one also recalls that all of these appearances occurred when man's knowledge was progressing by leaps and bounds, it becomes apparent that she is admonishing humanity to beware of knowledge which attempts to transcend God. An interesting aside is the effortlessness with which she traverses time and space while man struggles with cumbersome, complicated rockets and missiles for projected space travel.

There were varied physical phenomena associated with the different apparitions of Our Lady, but the most spectacular of all was a part of every one of these appearances. Without exception, Our Lady's appearances were accompanied by brilliant light—light of an unearthly intensity but which despite its brilliance did not hurt the eyes of those experiencing the vision. In the Fatima apparition, when Francisco was being questioned about the brightness of the Virgin, he was asked, "Which was brighter, the figure of the Virgin or the sun?" The answer was, "The figure of the Virgin was brighter." And of course it was at

Fatima that the sun performed its terrifying dance. At Guadalupe, Juan Diego speaks of the golden beams that rayed her from head to foot. St. Catherine Labouré says the angel who led her to the chapel "was surrounded with rays of light" and when describing Our Lady exclaims at "the beauty and the brilliance of the dazzling rays" that encompassed her. And so it was with every visitation. Brilliant, dazzling light of an unearthly quality bathed Mary in its rays.

All through the Bible from the creation of the world when God said, "Let there be light," light has been associated with God and His messengers. A cherubim with a flaming sword was placed before Paradise when Adam and Eve were cast out; when Moses received the Ten Commandments, lightning played around the mountaintop; the Holy Spirit appeared to the apostles as "tongues of fire"; and of course Our Lord Himself said, "I am the light of the world: he that followeth me, walketh not in darkness, but shall have the light of life" (John 8:12). These are just a few of the many references to light and its connection with God which constantly appear in the Bible. Through the ages men have always associated light with the forces of good. It is small wonder, then, that when Our Lady came from heaven to aid her children on earth a physical quality so closely connected with her Son was always present.

An interesting point might well be made here concerning Catholic teaching that Mary is the Mother of God. In the very first appearance here presented, in 1531, Mary says unequivocally, "I am the ever-virgin Mary, mother of the true God" and four centuries later at Beauraing she repeated "I am the Mother of God, the Queen of Heaven." It almost seems as if He is affirming to the world once again, by her appearances bathed in brilliant light, a quality so often associated with His Godship, that this is His mother and so the Mother of God.

Among Catholics it is basic teaching that Mary is the Mother of God. Obviously, if Mary is the Mother of Christ, which nobody denies, and if Christ is God, as all Christians believe, then it should naturally

follow that Mary must be the Mother of God. Despite the simple ratio-
nalization involved in this conclusion, many Christian sects deny that
Mary is the Mother of God. Here, in an obvious manner, through the
use of blinding light, He emphasizes this relationship and proclaims that
the Blessed Virgin, His mother, is the Mother of God.

Although not quite as universal as the light which invariably accompanied Our Lady's appearances, there is another physical characteristic
worthy of note. This is the prominent role the presence of water played
in so many of the apparitions. The spring at Lourdes is so famed that it is
hardly necessary to mention it; but Our Lady also caused springs to
appear at Banneux and La Salette; at Fatima a spring was found when
excavations were begun for the basilica in 1921 where water had never
before been found; and many of the other apparitions took place during
heavy rains. There seems to me a notable spiritual significance to the
combination of light, which is a property of fire, and water at these
apparitions. In the Old Testament, holocausts represented complete sacrifice to Almighty God for the Jews. In the New Testament, water is the
element used in Baptism which Christ instituted for the spiritual regen-
eration of all men. It would seem that the association of light and water
is symbolic of Our Lady's message calling for sacrifice and repentance
which will lead to salvation through her Son.

Another physical characteristic common to all of the apparitions is
that the Lady was always young and beautiful. In many cases, the visionaries become ecstatic in describing the beauty of the Lady. The slightest
reflection makes us realize that in these appearances Our Lady had to be
young and beautiful. As Eve, by her weakness, had been driven from
Paradise and by her sin had tainted the human race, so Mary offered to
the world the means of redemption through the fruit of her immaculate
body, Our Lord and Savior, Jesus Christ. This salvation is ever new,
ever fresh for all of mankind in all ages, in all places. Her youth in these
apparitions represents for mankind the fresh new life of salvation which

her Son constantly offers all men. (In the case of Guadalupe, as I have pointed out, I believe there is a further message to be found in the youth of the land in which the Lady appeared—a land which was to become a symbol of new hope for all mankind.) Man has the means for a rebirth; he has but to follow the path so clearly indicated to find a perpetual youth in life everlasting.

Just as she was young, so she was beautiful—and surpassingly beautiful she must have been. Truth, for which men have been searching for centuries, has an unmatched beauty, not merely in itself but because it is a reflection of the goodness of God who is Truth. Mary, as the Mother of God, shares this beauty, which, when revealed to earthlings, must dazzle them with its purity and beauty. And that is exactly how she appeared. Just as great artists through the centuries have tried in vain to capture the radiant, heavenly beauty of Our Lady, so these simple people graced by the visions of Our Lady tried to describe the beauty of this Lady—a beauty reflecting God—but could only say, as Bernadette said, that she was "a Lady, young and beautiful, exceedingly beautiful, the like of whom I had never seen." Nor had anyone else except those chosen few vouchsafed a glimpse of Heaven's glories with a vision of the Virgin.

Another physical property of the appearances worth noting was the fact that Our Lady always appeared clothed in white gowns of a dazzling and irresistible purity. The other colors most often associated with her visits were blue and gold, but always white predominated. The implication is so obvious that it hardly needs saying. White is a sign of purity, and Mary was the purest of all human beings that ever existed on earth. Conceived without sin, she remained a virgin throughout her life. The immaculate Conception and the Virgin Birth are mentioned in several of the apparitions and are constantly emphasized by the use of white in her clothing. Just as white is the obvious color for Our Lady's apparel, so, too, blue and gold are appropriate. For centuries gold has been our precious metal. What more fitting color to use for mankind's greatest treasure, Mary, man's intercessor with her beloved Son, than the color of His most precious commodity? By the same token, blue has always been regarded by mankind as the color of loyalty. What more effective, though subtle, manner of emphasizing that Our Lady demands complete loyalty of all of her children in the form of constant devotion and love of her beloved Son?

Before leaving this brief consideration of physical characteristics associated with the appearances, it might be well to note one other unusual feature. Many of the apparitions were witnessed under the most adverse conditions. It almost seemed as if the Devil was fighting a lost, rear-guard action to prevent Our Lady from delivering her message. On the night before the last great message at Fatima, all of Europe was swept by a storm of such intensity that William Thomas Walsh in his book on Our Lady says, "It was as if the devil, somewhere in the ice and snow that could never slake the burning of his pain, had resolved to destroy with one blow all that remained of the Europe which had so long been his battleground against the Thing he hated most." At Banneux several of the visions took place in driving rain and icy cold. At Lourdes, Bernadette was almost not allowed to go gather wood with her playmates because her mother felt it was too cold. At Knock, the apparition took place in a driving rain.

Interestingly enough, despite all these attempts, in many cases, the effects of nature invoked by diabolical powers—if this is the explanation—were immediately offset. For instance, at the last apparition at Fatima when the sun plummeted from the sky, a steady downpour preceded this phenomenon. When the sun had righted itself, everybody noticed that the clothes of all the spectators, more than 70,000 by unbiased reports, were completely dry. At Knock, despite a pouring rain, the ground immediately around the apparition area was completely dry. At Lourdes the water Bernadette had to cross was cold when she first crossed but warm on her return. It almost seemed as if the constant war between good and evil was waged by his Satanic Majesty down to the last second before he was forced to capitulate.

Important and interesting as all these considerations are, they fade into insignificance beside the importance and majesty of the message Our Lady is driving home to mankind. Over and over again she says the same thing. Repeatedly she admonishes, cajoles, and entreats us to listen to her. It almost seems that, Mother of mankind that she is, she is making a last desperate effort to save her beloved children. At La Salette she said, "If my people will not obey, I shall be compelled to loose my Son's arm. It is so heavy, so pressing that I can no longer restrain it. How long have I suffered for you! If my Son is not to cast you off, I am obliged to entreat Him without ceasing." Here is all the anguish and sorrow of a mother, deeply offended, but whose love for her children causes her to exert every effort to save them despite every rebuff.

Said in many different ways, the message, clear and direct, is simply that God is displeased with what has been going on on this earth. His patience is almost exhausted, and unless we listen to Him through His Blessed Mother He will wreak the vengeance which He has unleashed on the earth before. But it is far more than merely an admonishment to man to mend his way. Granted, she repeatedly tells the visionaries to spread the word that Our Lord is displeased and that men of all races must mend their ways, but she goes beyond this mere admonishment and tells us what we must do. Repeatedly she asks us to pray; repeatedly she begs us to do penance for our sins, and repeatedly she tells us that if we will do these things she will intercede with her Son for us.

Prayer, Penance, Reparation—these are the constant themes running through every message she has delivered. Though cast in a variety of forms, her demands are always the same. For example, she repeatedly asks the visionaries to build a shrine or a chapel or a church where she has appeared. But always she wants these shrines built not for her glory but for the worship and adoration of her Son. In return, a never-ending stream of graces and favors has poured forth from them. Who can ever estimate the benefits that have been bestowed upon mankind by the establishment of these centers of devotion and prayer at Lourdes, Fatima, La Salette, and the other places where her message has been heeded in this respect?

But like any good mother, she does more than plead with us; she does more than intercede for us; she does more than make promises. One has but to visit any of the great shrines erected at the sites of her apparitions and gaze upon the hundreds of abandoned crutches and listen to the stories of cures which have been effected to realize how faithfully Our Lady fulfills her promises. Perhaps no other fact has been so instrumental in impressing unbiased scientists of every creed, or even those of no belief, as the scrupulously compiled files and records of cures completely inexplicable to modern science. The thorough scientific investigator who is completely honest is the first to admit that these cases cannot be explained away by such glib explanations as hysteria, religious fervor, psychiatric phenomena, etc. The cases are there, they have been instantaneous and have continued over a long period of observed time. If, in a matter so inconsequential in the eternal plan of things, Our Lady proves her promises, how much more certain is it that we can depend completely and unreservedly on her greater promises?

In connection with these promises of Our Lady it is worth noting that in practically all of the apparitions many of these promises amounted to a prophecy. For example, she foretold to St. Catherine Labouré the tumultuous events in France in 1870, a prophecy which, as Father Dirvin points out, also anticipated the revolutions of 1830 and 1848. At La Salette she predicted great famine which soon materialized. And who can forget the chilling prediction at Fatima of World War II and the spread of Communism all over the world with its accompanying horror and terror?

History has shown that these prophecies have unerringly come true.

It is small wonder that her dramatic promise to convert Russia is of such tremendous significance and importance to the world today. With the development of modern thermonuclear devices capable of destroying the entire planet, it would seem impossible to conceive of a war between the two greatest powers on earth. Yet history shows time and again that the thought of death and destruction has never yet prevented war. When one considers the wars we have endured in the present century and the current state of world affairs, it is but natural to wonder what terrible fate is in store for the human race. But Our Lady holds out positive hope. "If my requests are heard, Russia will be converted and there will be peace." And even more decisively, "But in the end my Immaculate Heart will triumph." And, "I will convert sinners." With such promises, how unthinkable that man can refuse her wishes!

These are all matters affecting us as inhabitants of the earth, living our lives in a span of time. Far more important to all are those considerations affecting our eternal life. A cancer cured by the waters of Lourdes is a spectacular event. But as Christ so often pointed out, a physical cure shrinks into insignificance when compared to the cure of the soul.

Here Our Blessed Mother is no less emphatic than when she performed miraculous physical cures. "I will convert sinners," she said at Beauraing less than two decades after she had told Lucy at Fatima that "my Immaculate Heart will ever be your refuge and the way that will lead you to God." In short, what Mary, the Mother of God and Our Blessed Mother, is proposing in all these visitations is so stupendous that the human mind reels at the gigantic implications implicit in her promise. As the mother of us all she is offering to save the human race from its own folly and is pointing out to us the path we must follow to attain the salvation of our individual eternal souls. Small wonder she weeps so often in these appearances, when we stop to think that she did this some 2000 years ago when she brought forth into time on earth the eternal Word.

I will put enmity between you and the woman,
between your seed and her seed; He shall crush
your head, and you shall lie in wait for his heel.

GENESIS 3:15

Hail, full of grace, the Lord is with thee:
blessed art thou among women.

LUKE 1:28

And a great sign appeared in heaven: a woman
clothed with the sun, and the moon was under
her feet, and upon her head a crown of
twelve stars.

REVELATION 12:1

GUADALUPE

1531

OUR LADY OF
GUADALUPE IN MEXICO

Ethel Cook Eliot

Not such His dealings with any other nation.

PSALM 147:20

It happened on the arid top of a 130-foot hillock in wasteland five miles north of Mexico City, then confined to its original island in a lake. The date was Saturday, December 9, 1531; the hour, daybreak. Only one person witnessed it, however, and his account of the prodigy—until it was verified, four days later—was not believed.

It happened to a poor-as-poverty Aztec Indian. Born into the servant caste fifty-seven years earlier and given the Nahuatl name Singing Eagle, he had survived in obscurity the Spanish conquest of 1519–21. Until the truth of his strange tale had been sealed with a visible, durable sign, he had been of no account to anyone in this world except his no-account friends and family. When he did become of immense account to millions, almost overnight (and without benefit of radio or television), his wife had been dead for several years and they had had no children. His one remaining relative was an uncle—an uncle who had been his foster father since early childhood. Uncle and nephew had been among the first Indians to be converted to Christianity by the Franciscan missionaries, who baptized them with the names they had gone by for the past seven years—Juan Bernardino and Juan Diego.

Juan Diego was devoted to his old uncle, but their relationship was by this time turned about: Juan Diego was watching over the old man with as much care as he had received from him fifty years ago. They lived near each other, but alone, in Tolpetlac, a village of one-room houses thatched with cornstalks. In spite of the task of growing corn and beans for them both, and hiring himself out for any other labor he could get, Juan Diego managed to see his uncle and be of help to him at some time every day. But this Saturday, December 9, was unprecedented. Juan Bernardino had no sight of his nephew all that day.

Juan Diego had left the village before daybreak in order to be in time to hear the Mass celebrated in Our Lady's honor (as the Franciscans then did on Saturdays) at the church of Santiago in the village of Tlaltelolco. It was a long run over the hills, and the Fathers stressed the importance of never coming to a Mass late, and called the roll of their converts before beginning. Running through the high, rare air in the hardy Indian manner, he would have arrived at the same hour as any other morning if he hadn't been halted in his tracks by what he took for a burst of bird song. This was unheard-of, at this time of year, with everything so bleak and cold. Even at the appropriate season, Juan had never before heard birds welcome the dawn with an abrupt burst into song all together. The music was thrillingly sharp, and thrillingly sweet. As it went on, Juan's ear discerned what seemed a harmony among separate choirs of song birds scattered over the scrubby sides of a little hill that his path skirted. On this hill, Tepeyac, had formerly stood a temple to the Mother-goddess of the Aztecs. Now it was desert.

Quite soon the shrill caroling stopped as suddenly as it had begun, with no lingering twitters. Such a silence with no breath of warning unnerved Juan. He didn't resume running. He stood listening to the silence, straining for some sound, any sound to break the spell. It came almost at once, but it was as astounding in that place and at that time as the bird music had been. A woman was calling down to him from the ruinous rocks at the top of Tepeyac hill. Though day had broken, Juan couldn't see her. A frosty mist, a brightening cloud hid the rocks and the woman who was calling. She was calling him by name, and urgently: "Juan! Juan Diego! Juanito! Juan Dieguito!"

Whoever she was, he must go up to her and find out what she wanted of him. It was a short climb to the top, but he got no sight of her until he reached the rocks, and then he saw her more completely than he had ever seen anything else in his life. He saw what he looked at, whole and at the same time in the minutest detail.

The sun wasn't above the horizon, yet Juan saw her as if against the sun because of the golden beams that rayed her person from head to feet. She was a young Mexican girl about fourteen years old and wonderfully beautiful. Her garments were wonderfully beautiful. The rocks and dry grasses and stunted thorn trees were wonderfully beautiful, as if her splendor radiated onto them. The cactus leaves gleamed like emeralds, and their spines like gold. Each plant, each stone was sharply etched on Juan's vision, transparent and jewel-like in color. But Juan was not dazzled by the radiance before him and all around him. It was just the opposite. He saw it all with heightened powers of vision, and when the girl finally spoke, he heard with the same heightened power of hearing every most delicate inflection and emphasis of his mother tongue. *"Nopiltzin, campa tiauh?"*

The girl said: "Juan, smallest and dearest of my little children, where were you going?"

Juan said: "My lady and my child,[1] I was hurrying to Tlaltelolco to see the Mass and hear the Gospel explained."

The girl said: "Dear little son, I love you. I want you to know who I am. I am the ever-virgin Mary, Mother of the true God who gives life and maintains it in existence. He created all things. He is in all places. He is lord of heaven and earth. I desire a *teocali* (temple or church) at this place where I will show my compassion to your people and to all people who sincerely ask my help in their work and in their sorrows. Here, I will see their tears; I will console them and they will be at ease. So run now to Tenochtitlán (Mexico City) and tell the Lord Bishop all that you have seen and heard."

Juan had fallen to his knees when the Virgin told him who she was. Now he prostrated himself at her feet and said, "Noble Lady, I will do what you ask of me!" Then he quickly rose and took courteous and humble leave of her.

This was no light service. If anyone else, no matter how exalted a person, had directed Juan Diego to take a message to the Bishop in the city and deliver it to him personally, Juan would have made every excuse possible to get out of it. The five-mile run to the city was no great matter. He was fifty-seven years old and fasting since yesterday's sunset, but his body was agile and toughened from early childhood. Indians of Juan's low degree, however, seldom went into Mexico City, and Juan had never had the temerity to do so, even before the Spanish conquest.

[1] This "child," and the other diminutives used by Juan at later meetings, appear in the oldest account. Probably Aztecs of Juan's servant caste habitually used them toward their superiors; but we may also remember that the Virgin looked young enough to be Juan's granddaughter.

The Spaniards in Tlaltelolco were different. Even the Indians who held fast to their forefathers' beliefs—and these were still the vast majority—didn't think of the Franciscan missionaries as their conquerors. They and their converts together had built the church there and a school and a many-roomed house for themselves. To even the humblest, they seemed fellow men—poor, roughly clothed in brown tunics, hardworking, meagerly fed, and serenely gentle. So Juan felt as easy in Tlaltelolco as he did in Tolpetlac. But Tenochtitlán! And even if the Spanish hidalgos and soldiers he would run into there didn't set their dogs on him or beat him, how was he to find his way to the Bishop's house? He was badly frightened.

However much trouble Juan may have gone through before he arrived at the door of the palace, he did manage it, was admitted inside, and after some rough treatment from the servants that just fell short of injury to his person, and being kept waiting in a corner for a very long time, he found himself at last in the episcopal presence.

The Bishop-elect (not yet consecrated) was Don Fray Juan de Zumárraga, a Franciscan who, in Spain, had distributed a royal gift to his community among poor laymen, thus winning the king's notice and the papal appointment. In Mexico since 1528, he had greatly softened the conquerors' harshness to the Indians. It was not he who had kept Juan waiting all those hours; he had only now been told that a lowly native from the country was there with a message for his ear alone, and would let no one else relay it.

The Lord Bishop was courteous and kind in his reception of Juan Diego. (It is hardly probable that the Aztec could speak enough Spanish to convey Our Lady's message, but the Bishop kept an interpreter, Juan González, who had come to Mexico with Cortés, presently became a missionary, and in 1534 a priest.) Listening to the story, the Bishop was impressed by the Indian's humility and seeming sincerity. He asked Juan a few questions—where he lived, his occupation, his knowledge of the

Gospels, his religious practices—and he found Juan's responses satisfactory. But the story of that encounter and dialogue with the Queen of Heaven, and how she desired a church built in that uninhabited place— he shook his head. He ended the interview by saying he would think it over. Juan could come again, if he cared to, and they would talk further about it.

The sun was almost set when Juan came back to the hill where he had heard the strange bird choirs and seen the radiant little Virgin. Tired and very hungry as he must have been by this time, he swerved from the path and climbed to the spot. Though he had sadly failed the Mother of God in the matter of her new temple, holy ground was holy ground. He must do it reverence.

When he reached the top, the Blessed Virgin was there, waiting for him as if it had been arranged between them. Juan knelt down. He said: "My dearest child, my Lady and Queen, I did your errand. I told the Bishop all that I had seen and heard here. He listened, and asked many questions; but I could see he did not believe that everything was just as I said it was. He thought I could be mistaken about your wanting a church in this waste place, and even about who it was I had seen and spoken with here. He gave me kind permission to visit him again, but I fear I should get no further. I am not worthy of your trusting me with a message so important. Please send someone more suitable; for I am a nobody . . . Forgive my boldness in advising you."

The Blessed Virgin said: "Listen, little son. There are many I could send. But you are the one I have chosen for this task. So, tomorrow morning, go back to the Bishop. Tell him it is the Virgin Mary who sends you, and repeat to him my great desire for a church in this place."

Juan said: "I will do so willingly, though I fear the Bishop may not be pleased to see me back so soon. And if he is pleased, he still may not believe that it was really you who sent me. But I am your servant and will obey your every wish. Tomorrow I will return here to tell you how my second try comes out. So, youngest of my daughters, Noble Lady, rest yourself until then."

The next morning, Sunday, Juan rose in the dark and got to the church in Tlaltelolco in time for Mass. Directly Mass was over, he went on into Mexico City to confront the Bishop a second time. The palace servants had perhaps been rebuked, for they let him in with almost no ado, and one of them went promptly off to announce him.

Fray Juan de Zumárraga was astonished and possibly annoyed. It was true he had told the visionary Indian to come again, if he wished, at some later date, but that he was here the very next day and so early in the morning—that seemed hysterical or, at the least, childish. Busy as he was, however, the Bishop received him with outward patience and listened to his tale of a second meeting with the Blessed Virgin, up where the rocks were, on little Tepeyac.

Juan related how, much to his surprise, the Queen of angels and men had waited all yesterday in that lonely place to learn what the Bishop meant to do about the church she wanted built there. But when he, poor Juan Diego, had the boldness to inform her that the Bishop seemed uncertain it was she herself who had sent the message, she had not shown dismay. She had simply said that Juan should return this morning and assure the Bishop it *was* she herself—the ever-Virgin—and that she *did* desire a building in that place.

The Bishop was thoughtful. He was beginning almost to believe that this simple Indian might not be deluded. But there are visions and visions; some are heavenly, some are not, no matter how much they assume the disguise of holiness. He no longer wondered whether this earnest convert had perhaps made up the story for vanity's sake or to gain something practical for himself, such as having a church built nearer his own village for his better convenience in getting to Mass.

Even with ulterior motives for fabricating his meetings with Nuestra Señora, this poor Indian was far too simple for so impressive a performance. Moreover, everything about the story was so circumstantial! No matter how closely the man was questioned or asked to repeat any part of description or dialogue, he never contradicted himself. Rather, it seemed as if the questions brought to his mind such trivial points as he would not think of inventing. Still, there was nothing, as yet, that Bishop Zumárraga could act on. Some proof that Juan, however truthful, was not suffering deception or delusion, was indispensable—but what sort of proof?

In the end the Bishop rather tentatively suggested that Juan might ask Santa Maria for a sign that would prove it was truly herself. Juan was going right back to her on the little hill . . . ? Very well—

But before dismissing Juan, the Bishop left the room for a few moments to instruct two of his most trusted servants to follow the Indian home. They were to keep far enough behind him not to let him realize he was being followed; to notice very carefully any persons he stopped to speak with; and to watch him until he reached his village, no matter how far away that was.

These two servants returned with their report much sooner than the Bishop had expected them. The distressing thing was that the Indian had outwitted them, or that was the excuse they offered. Passing through the city, he spoke to no one nor did anyone so much as greet him. Outside the city, he quickened his pace, but they kept him in sight. He was on the road ahead of them until he reached the foot of a little hill about five miles out. At that point he simply vanished. They searched the whole vicinity, but he was too cleverly hidden; they couldn't find him.

But Juan had not outwitted anyone, nor been clever at hiding. He had not been aware that he was under surveillance. He could see the top of the Virgin's hill. He could be seen from it. That was his goal, and his only thought the thought of who was watching for him up there among the rocks.

Again Juan knelt at the feet of holy Mary and told her how the Bishop had asked for a sign. This did not discompose her; in fact, she appeared pleased. She said: "Very well, little son. Come back tomorrow at daybreak. I will give you a sign for him. You have taken much trouble on my account, and I shall reward you for it. Go in peace, and rest."

But the next thing was for Juan to visit his uncle, and it was well he did. The old man had been stricken with *cocolistle*, a contagious and deadly fever that Juan recognized only too well. He gathered herbs and prepared medicines. He kept up his own strength with food. Through that night and the day and night following, he did everything that was humanly possible to relieve Juan Bernardino's sufferings. He did not keep his appointment with the Virgin that Monday morning, but gave precedence to his uncle's need.

Sometime before daybreak on Tuesday, Juan Bernardino took a turn for the worse. He felt certain that he would not live to see the sun set that day, and begged his nephew to run to Tlaltelolco and return with a priest. The only service Juan could render him now, and the last one in this world, was to arrange that he should not die without receiving the Last Sacraments. No matter how lonely and uncared-for Juan left his dear foster father, this duty came first for them both.

This time on his run to Tlaltelolco, Juan chose to go round the east side of Tepeyac hill. It was on the west side that the Blessed Virgin had first seen him and called him up to her. If she were there now she would see him again, for day was just breaking. She might call him again. This would mean delay, when every moment was precious.

But it didn't work. He was hardly started on the eastern path when he saw her descending Tepeyac at an angle that would intercept him just beyond the next curve. He couldn't turn back. She must have seen him, and would be astonished if he were so discourteous as to avoid the meeting. He did not slow his pace until he was near enough to kneel at her feet.

She said: "Least of my sons, what is the matter?"

And as if to make light of his embarrassment he answered at first: "My dear child, my Lady! Why are you up so early? Are you well?" But then (and how breathless the words must have sounded), "Forgive me! My uncle is dying of *cocolistle* and desires me to fetch a priest to give him the Last Sacraments. It was no heedless promise I made to meet you yesterday morning and take the Bishop the sign you intended to send him. But my uncle fell ill."

The Blessed Virgin said: "My little son. Do not be distressed and afraid. Am I not here who am your Mother? Are you not under my shadow and protection? Your uncle will not die at this time. This very moment his health is restored. There is no reason now for the errand you set out on, and you can peacefully attend to mine. Go up to the top of the hill; cut the flowers that are growing there and bring them to me."

No flowers could be in bloom on the frozen hill. Nor could Juan's uncle be healed of his wasting sickness and be, all in one moment, perfectly well. But Juan did not question the Blessed Virgin's words. Nor was it blind faith that made him believe. He was seeing her, hearing her voice.

Castilian roses—exotic, impossible—were growing on the hilltop. Juan noticed as he cut them that their petals were drenched with dew, not rimed with frost as the scrub and mesquite were. The best way to protect them against the cold was to cradle them in his *tilma*—a regular Aztec garment like a long cape worn in front, and often looped up as a carryall. Not to tire the Blessed Virgin with further waiting, Juan worked quickly, filling his *tilma* with the fresh, fragrant blossoms. Then he ran down and, bending low before her, held out the slightly opened wrap for her to see that this time, anyway, he had been successful in fulfilling her desire. But he had dropped the flowers helter-skelter into the fold, and the Virgin was not satisfied. With her own holy hands she rearranged them carefully, taking thought over every rose as to just how it should lie. Then she tied the lower corners of his *tilma* behind his neck, so that nothing could spill.

When she was done she said, "You see, little son, this is the sign I am sending to the Bishop. Tell him that now he has his sign, he should build the temple I desire in this place. Do not let anyone but him see what you are carrying. Hold both sides until you are in his presence and have already told him how I intercepted you on your way to fetch a priest to give the Last Sacraments to your uncle, how I assured you he was perfectly healed and sent you up to cut these roses, and myself arranged them like this. Remember, little son, that you are my trusted ambassador, and this time the Bishop will believe all that you tell him."

As far as is known, this was the last time here on earth that Juan Diego ever saw the Virgin or heard her voice.

All the way to the Bishop's palace Juan delighted in the perfume of the roses. He held his *tilma* tightly closed, but their fragrance penetrated the coarse weave and scented the winter air he ran through. The palace servants when Juan gained admittance were astonished by the sweet odor that entered along with the beggarly Indian. They traced it to what he was so craftily hiding from them in his uncouth apron. When Juan refused to let them see, or tell them anything, they jostled and startled him in hope to loosen his grip enough for a glimpse. They succeeded, but could hardly believe their eyes. Some snatched at the flowers, but each time a rose was touched it no longer seemed real but rather an embroidery or painting on the cream-colored cloth. Word of the commotion soon reached the Bishop, and Juan was fetched away to his apartment.

This time several of the Bishop's household were present. Perhaps he had summoned them to give their various opinions of this vision-seeing Indian.

Juan unhaltingly advanced and stood before the episcopal chair. Lest he loose his clutch on the sides of his *tilma*, he dared not kneel down as courtesy demanded. So he stood all the minutes it took to tell what the Blessed Virgin had urgently requested he should tell and in the right order. He added nothing and left out nothing. Sentence by sentence, Juan González interpreted. Then Juan Diego put up both hands and untied the corners of crude cloth behind his neck. The looped-up fold of the *tilma* fell; the flowers he thought were the precious sign tumbled out and lay in an untidy heap on the floor. Alas for the Virgin's careful arrangement!

But Juan's confusion over this mishap was nothing to what he felt immediately after it. Inside of seconds the Bishop had risen from his chair and was kneeling at Juan's feet, and inside of a minute all the other persons in the room had surged forward and were also kneeling. Juan would have thought they were praying except that he himself seemed the object of their rapt gazes. But no, it was his *tilma*, that now hung down to his ankles.

No wonder the Bishop and his household were kneeling before that length of primitive cloth. Millions of people have knelt before it since, in awe and gratitude as profound as theirs who saw it first. The miracle of the roses was sign enough of the authenticity of the Indian's visions, but the Blessed Virgin had trusted him with an even more wonderful sign. What she had imprinted on his vision and memory at the time of the first apparition, now—three days later—was imaged in glorious beauty on the front of his *tilma*.

However long the Bishop and the others with him knelt in reverent awe before this first showing of the miraculous picture, the moment came when he rose, gently untied the *tilma* of the astounded Indian, lifted it from him, and carried it with all reverence into his private chapel. There, after it was appropriately attached to a wall near the altar, Juan himself could kneel with the others in prolonged and prayerful wonder.

Juan was willing to remain in the palace for the rest of that day and the night following. He had no anxiety about his uncle's health, and the Bishop requested his continued presence. Meanwhile, the news spread. Early Wednesday morning Juan's humble *tilma*, glorified by the supernatural image imprinted on it, was carried in solemn and joyous procession to the cathedral, where everyone in the city thronged to see it and pray before it.

The next thing was for Juan to show to the Bishop and those he asked to accompany them the sacred hill where the Blessed Virgin desired a church to be built. After viewing the holy ground—bleak now and with no traces of the glory that had so recently blessed it—the Bishop gave Juan permission to return to his village. He himself would waste no time about constructing at least a shrine on Tepeyac, but some of his company could go with the Indian to see how his uncle fared, and if he was well enough they were to bring him back with Juan to Mexico City.

Juan Bernardino was sunning himself at his door when his nephew arrived, and was astonished by his escort of friars and *caballeros*. He wasn't in custody; he was showing them the way. Rapidly the villagers were closing in around them, forgetting timidity in their eagerness to see and hear Juan Diego's amazement at finding his uncle alive and well. All yesterday they had looked for his return with a priest. By last night they felt sure he had himself come down with the dread *cocolistle*. Now today he appeared with a whole troop of Fathers and hidalgos!

Encircled by the fascinated audience, uncle and nephew were embracing. Juan Diego was eager to give his uncle the joyous explanation of his long absence, but in courtesy he first inquired how he felt now; and the old man had his own marvels of yesterday morning to relate. Too weak even to drink the concoction of herbs his nephew had left at his side, he longed for daylight and spiritual comfort, yet had no hope of living until either could arrive. Darkness encompassed him, when of a sudden the room filled with soft light. A luminous young woman, all made of peace and love, stood beside him. She told him he would get well, and he believed her. She told him she had intercepted his nephew and sent him to the Bishop with a picture of herself to be enshrined at Tepeyac. She further told him, "Call me and call my image Santa María de Guadalupe." Then she disappeared, and dawn stole in.

(Now Guadalupe—the "river of the wolf" in Saracenic Spain—had given its name to a little statue of Madonna and Child which a cowherd found buried near it, toward the end of the thirteenth century when the Moors had been expelled from Estremadura. King Alfonso XI enshrined it in a chapel. Columbus prayed there before his voyage and named one of the Antilles he discovered "Guadalupe." To the Spaniards in Mexico the name seemed natural. Applying it to the Indian Virgin made them feel at home in New Spain. But to the natives it could have no appeal. They could not even pronounce it, for neither G nor D (nor R) is used in Nahuatl. "Santa Malía," as they pronounced María, was familiar to them, especially to converts like Juan Bernardino, but instead of "de Guadalupe" some other, more intelligible, syllables must have been spoken to him by the Apparition. Recent research, especially that of Helen Behrens, strongly suggests that these were *tetlcoatlax-opeuh*, which when repeated by Juan Bernardino to the Spaniards were heard as "de Guatlashupe," easily assimilated by their ears to the Old World title. Of course they supposed the old Indian was doing his best to say "de Guadalupe"! But to all Aztec ears the compound epithet meant Stone Serpent Troddenon: the Apparition had announced that she had suppressed and supplanted Quetzalcoatl, the terrible god (originally perhaps a comet, later the planet nearest earth) idolized as a feathered serpent, to whom countless men had been excruciatingly sacrificed. What wonder that as the word spread among the Indians of *this* title given to herself by the vision of Juan Bernardino *and* the promise made by the identical vision to Juan Diego ("I will give motherly love and compassion to all who seek my aid"), plus the actual picture in which they could read many concurrent symbols—clouds, sun, stars, crescent, and the little black cross on a golden brooch—the natives swarmed to embrace the Christian religion in which one divine man had been sacrificed once and for all. The Mother of this God had come to them directly and told them in their own tongue that she had trodden on the serpent's head.

In the seven years 1532–38, *eight million* natives were baptized. Friar Toribio de Benavente recorded that in five days, 14,500 presented themselves at his mission and were anointed with oil and chrism. Learning of the sacrament of matrimony, 1000 couples were married in one day. For Easter, 1540, twelve different tribes peacefully assembled at one church, some from as far away as 150 miles. Today over five million people come annually to Guadalupe, and the descendants of the Aztecs, dancing, hail "Teotl Inantzin" (God's Mother) by her title, "Coatlalupej," and sing how "She freed us from great evil, She crushed the serpent!")

This, to Juan Bernardino, was the fifth apparition of our Holy Mother on the American continent—a delicate kindness shown to her Juanito's foster father. Through him she made known to Spaniard and to

Aztec the significant name by which her image was to unify them in Christendom.

Juan Bernardino got up and went about his chores, serene and well. Not until this morning had he begun to worry over his nephew's long absence. What, now, had kept him, and why were all these white men so respectful? Never had he seen such a novelty—not in his lifetime. It nearly overwhelmed him when he was placed upon a litter, and four young men of Tolpetlac were hired to bear him to the Bishop's palace. To the City in the Lake! For a fortnight's visit!

Swiftly news of the church to be built in the precinct of the Mother-goddess on Tepeyac was carried from village to village. The Indians' own church, requested through one of themselves! Volunteer laborers appeared, more than could be employed. In only thirteen days the simple chapel-like structure was completed. On the day after Christmas the sacred Image was brought to it in a great procession and installed above the altar; the church was blessed and the Mass celebrated.

Here ends the earliest account (c.1560) of these miracles, written in Nahuatl by an Aztec of the former imperial family who was educated at Tlaltelolco and attained very high office under the name of Don Antonio Valeriano (died 1605). But recently there came to light a much older, actually contemporary document that had lain among the Archives of the Indies in Seville, Spain. This is a letter to the conqueror Cortés, written by Bishop Zumárraga on Christmas Eve, 1531. It presupposes Cortés' acquaintance with recent events and is not explicit, but it is imbued with exaltation.

I have had the news published—sent a messenger to Cuernavaca—an Indian to Fray Toribio—am preparing the festival and keeping with me a little longer your honor's trumpeters. How glorious it will be! The joy of

all is indescribable. Tell my lady the Marquesa [Cortés' wife] that even-
tually I want to dedicate my cathedral to the Immaculate Conception
because it was during that feast [December 8–17 in the missal used in
Mexico] that God and his Blessed Mother deigned to shower the land you
won with this great favor. No more now.

The Bishop Elect, filled with joy.

Cortés and his marquesa took part in the procession. Everybody walked in it. But the Indians danced too, and one in his frenzy was grievously wounded by an arrowhead piercing his neck. Unconscious, he was laid before the Image, and amid fervent prayers a friar staunched his wound. His eyes opened. He beheld the Image. He revived. He lived. And the Aztec hymns rose louder than before. "The chiefs sing to thee, Santa María, the people dance before thee. Speak, Father Bishop, to us thy children, newborn beside the lake."

While the millions of baptisms were taking place, Juan Diego spent his days in a hermitage built for him beside the little chapel on the holy hill. To pilgrims he showed the sacred picture and repeated the story. At a time when the laity was not accustomed to frequent communion, he, by special order of the Bishop, received his Savior three times a week. When he died in 1548, his room, appropriately, became the baptistry of "the old church of the Indians," and on one wall of it a tablet proclaimed, "In this place Our Lady of Guadalupe appeared to an Indian named Juan Diego who is buried in this church." Juan Bernardino, too, was reverenced, and after he died in 1544 his hut in Tolpetlac became a chapel that still stands, in good repair. In 1545 a cruel pestilence abated when the small children of the countryside were brought together before the Virgin's picture and appealed to her.

Not quite a century after the miracles of 1531, Mexico City was badly flooded during four years of unusual rain. In a convent there an Indian lay sister had a vision of the Virgin as portrayed on the *tilma*, propping up the threatened walls. Accordingly, the Archbishop with a rich flotilla of boats, lights, and music fetched the precious Image from Tepeyac to its "birthplace" in his palace, and kept it in the capital till the floods subsided. In 1663 it left the original shrine for a stately, towered temple built for it close by, where it was kept locked in a silver tabernacle and behind curtains except during Mass or when responsible persons were present. Only forty-six years later (1709) it was installed in its present place, around which a complex of buildings grew. Eventually, in 1904, the great, domed church was declared a basilica; and since its interior was done over in 1931 it has been considered the most beautiful church in the Western Hemisphere.

Above the high altar is Juan Diego's *tilma*—still intact. Two straight pieces, coarsely woven of fiber from the maguey plant, are sewn together so that the whole measures 66 inches by 41 inches. In color it looks rather like unbleached linen. Modern scientists are agreed that in the Mexican climate this cloth would naturally have disintegrated beyond recognition within twenty years. On its fishnet-like web no painting could ever have been done; and even on a properly prepared canvas the picture would within two hundred years have been browned over to the point of obliteration. What colors, what gilt were employed is still a mystery. The technique has eluded and still eludes all endeavors to elucidate it.

The figure is only 56 inches tall, but as one draws back from it, it seems to become larger and more plastic. Surrounded by golden rays, it emerges as from a shell of light, clear-cut and lovely in every detail of line and color. The head is bent slightly and very gracefully to the right, just avoiding the long seam. The eyes look downward, but the pupils are visible. This gives an unearthly impression of lovingness and lovableness. The mantle that covers the head and falls to the feet is greenish blue with a border of purest gold, and scattered through with golden stars. The tunic is rose-colored, patterned with a lace-like design of golden flowers. Below is a crescent moon, and beneath it appear the head and arms of a cherub. Although he is tiny in size, he seems to be balancing the image above him with joyous ease.

The seer saw the Blessed Virgin as a person of his own race, and was firm in this conviction. Her physiognomy in the painting bears him out, as also do her garments. Her star-studded outer mantle resembles that of an Aztec queen. In so appearing she showed herself a mother to him and to his people in a most especial way; but the picture's expression is archetypical of adorable motherhood in every race of man.

As recently as 1921 the Image was preserved as if by Our Lady's special watchfulness from the persecutors of the Church who then ran the Mexican government. They did not dare to close the basilica, so beloved by the Indian masses, but someone hid a bomb in a bunch of flowers at the altar, timed to explode at the climax of a pontifical high Mass. Most of the hierarchy, as well as the Image, would be within its range. The bomb went off, shattering an altarpiece and twisting a big bronze cross, but not a man was hurt and the glass in front of the Image did not even crack.

The frames surrounding the sacred picture and the various jeweled crowns above it are brilliant with earthly splendor. But the splendor of the Image is not of this earth, not of man's making. The eyes that gaze on it now see it exactly as Bishop Zumárraga and the others saw it when the roses spilled from Juan's mantle and it was first revealed. Millions have viewed it during the four and a quarter centuries since. At the present time, some fifteen hundred persons kneel before it on every ordinary day, and on days of pilgrimages (of which there are many, every year, from other countries) the numbers cannot be counted.

The Feast of Our Lady of Guadalupe is the Patronal Festivity of Mexico and is also celebrated with solemnity in the Southwest of the United States. To all American Indians, we may suppose, the message applies as it was spoken: an end to strife and cruelty, a promise of solace, peace, maternal love. To all inhabitants of the Americas, the Image implies a unity of brothers, a union of races acknowledging the fatherhood of God. The Mother of the Incarnation of God made it and gave it to us all, to reaffirm and vivify the pivotal point of the Creed: that her Son was true God and true man, Redeemer and Savior.

We cannot know how long this Holy Image will remain, nor how long this earth of ours will endure, but the effect of Our Lady's appearances and gift is continuous, and God may mean the Western Hemisphere to play a special part in these latter days by exemplifying, defending, and spreading His purposes for all mankind.

PARIS

1830

THE LADY
OF THE
MIRACULOUS
MEDAL

Rev. Joseph I. Dirvin, C.M.

The pagan world into which Our Lady was born had no knowledge of her coming, nor of the new day she heralded. It was much the same in 1806 when Catherine Labouré was born. She was a nobody, a country child, hidden in a pocket of the Burgundian hills. The brilliant skeptical world of Voltaire, the proud world of Napoléon Bonaparte, would have snubbed her. Yet she heralded a new Marian day, a day of such duration that it would be called the Age of Mary.

Catherine Labouré was born on May 2, 1806 in the tiny village of Fain-les-moutiers, not far from Dijon. Her father, Pierre Labouré, was easily the most important man in the village, for he owned the biggest farm. He was an educated man, having studied for the priesthood in his youth, and had added to his dignity by marrying Madeleine Louise Gontard, a former school mistress, whose family were minor country gentry. Pierre and Madeleine were perfect complements; he was a gruff, silent man with an iron will which brooked no interference; she was reserved and gentle.

Catherine was the ninth of eleven children, but for all practical purposes, during her growing-up years her younger sister Marie Antoinette, or Tonine, seems to have been the only one of her brothers and sisters whose life was bound up with hers.

Catherine's mother was the source of her sanctity; Tonine was the friend and confidante of her childhood and adolescence. Madame Labouré seems to have had second sight concerning Catherine's destiny, for she took pains to instill in her a special love of God and to place her in the ways of holiness. She succeeded so well that upon her death, when Catherine was only nine years old, the little girl was prepared to go on alone. In the midst of her terrible grief at her mother's passing, Catherine turned to Our Lady. Climbing up on a chair, she reached for a statue of the Blessed Virgin that stood high on a shelf in her mother's bedroom, clasped it to her breast, and said aloud:

"Now, dear Blessed Mother, you will be my mother."

This remarkable incident, with its hint of irrevocable dedication, truly marks the start of the Marian Age. That the child meant what she said is evident from the deepening of her spiritual life. During the next two years, she and Tonine lived with a kindly aunt, Marguerite Jeanrot, her father's sister, in the nearby village of Saint-Rémy. Here there was a resident priest, a boon which Fain did not have, and for the first time in her life Catherine was given an organized course of instruction in Catholic doctrine and spiritual practice. It was the only formal education she was to receive, a strange and mysterious thing, for she came of educated parents and her brothers and sisters all had schooling in varying degrees. It is hard not to see here the design of heaven to keep Catherine ignorant, so that the divine origin of her visions, with their accurate delineation of deep doctrine, might be the more apparent. At Saint-Rémy, Catherine began to prepare for her first Communion and to withdraw more and more from the playful life of childhood into a solemnity beyond her years. "She had no time for games," was the way Tonine put it; and again: "From the time of her first Communion, she became entirely mystic."

At this point her father suddenly called Catherine and Tonine home and turned over to Catherine the running of his household. It was a tremendous task, and many an older woman would have balked at it. Besides her father, there were three brothers and a sister still at home for Catherine to care for, and one of these, the youngest, was an invalid, who required constant nursing. There were fourteen hired men, whose dinner must be carried to them in the fields. There was all the attendant cooking and cleaning and sewing. It meant late to bed and early to rise for this little girl—she was no more than that.

Yet she found time for a more or less formal religious life. Each morning Catherine walked some six miles in the predawn darkness to Mass. Throughout the day she managed to slip away to the village chapel across the lane from her home; there her favorite devotion was to kneel in prayer before a battered old painting of the Annunciation.

At the age of eighteen Catherine had her first mystical experience. It was in the form of a dream, wherein she found herself assisting at the Mass of an old priest, who was a stranger to her. At the end of Mass he turned and beckoned to her, but she fled in fright. Then, in her dream, Catherine went to visit a sick neighbor, only to encounter the same venerable priest. As she turned to flee from him the second time, he called after her:

"You do well to visit the sick, my child. You flee from me now, but one day you will be glad to come to me. God has plans for you; do not forget it."

Catherine was not to know the meaning of this dream until four years later.

In the meantime she began to clear the way toward a religious vocation by training Tonine to take over the household. Catherine refused at least three proposals of marriage, only to meet with a flat "no" from her father when she asked his permission to enter religion. Indeed, he took positive steps to prevent her, sending her to Paris to serve as a waitress in her brother's café, with the thought that the allurements of the city might distract her from her religious purpose. After a year of the deepest misery Catherine managed to escape, with the connivance of her brothers and sisters, to a fashionable finishing school conducted by a sister-in-law at Châtillon.

Here Catherine was forced to endure the ridicule of her schoolmates, for her ignorance was truly abysmal. In spite of private tutoring from her sister-in-law, Catherine learned next to nothing, for she had no interest in the world or its niceties of learning. Châtillon, however, was to remain blessed in her memory, for in this ancient town she found her vocation: it was in the visitor's parlor of the Hôpital de Saint-Sauveur in Châtillon that Catherine recognized the old priest of her dream in a portrait of St. Vincent de Paul and knew that God meant her to be a Sister of Charity.

Although Catherine's calling was now crystal-clear, nevertheless, she had serious obstacles to overcome before she would be free to follow that calling. First, there was her father. Catherine was twenty-three years old and did not need her father's permission to enter religion, but obedience was the soul of her spiritual life, and she felt that her obedience would not be perfect, should she not have his blessing. Her sister-in-law Jeanne Labouré came to her assistance. Jeanne was a favorite with the crusty old man and could bend him to her will. He gave in, at last, to her blandishments and sent Catherine the blessing she so desperately wanted, but, in doing so, thrust one final barb into her heart. He refused her the dowry customarily required of those entering the Sisterhood. It was a stupid thing to do, for it only served to humiliate the daughter who had served him so well, and to reveal his own meanness. Catherine showed her mettle, however, uttering never a word of criticism or complaint—in fact, all her life she spoke of her father in the most glowing terms. Jeanne and her husband, Catherine's brother Hubert, supplied the dowry and the trousseau Catherine would need.

The second obstacle to Catherine's vocation was more difficult to remove. The Sister Superior of the hospital at Châtillon was most reluctant to receive a religious candidate so poorly educated as Catherine. Once more, Catherine found a champion, this time in the person of the Sister Assistant of the house, Sister Victoire Séjole. Catherine had been accompanying Sister Séjole on her errands of mercy, and the good Sister, who had an extraordinary faculty for discerning souls, had come to recognize in her an unusual depth of spirituality. She begged the Superior to accept the girl, pointing out that Catherine was "a good village girl, the kind St. Vincent loved," and promising to instruct her personally in the rudiments of learning she would need. The Sister Superior acquiesced, and Catherine found herself in the possession of the only way of life she had ever wanted.

She entered the Sisters of Charity as a postulant at Châtillon on January 22, 1830, and in the scant three months she spent there left an unforgettable impression of goodness. On April 21, 1830, she entered the novitiate, or seminary, as the Sisters of Charity call it, at 140 rue du Bac in Paris. She arrived just in time to assist at the translation of the body of St. Vincent de Paul from the Cathedral of Notre Dame to the newly erected mother church of the Vincentian Fathers. A novena of thanksgiving was held at the church to celebrate this great event, and each evening, on returning home, Catherine was granted a vision of St. Vincent's heart.

These visions were truly a prelude to the great apparitions of Our

Lady soon to come. They were the first of a train of miraculous favors Catherine was to receive all her life. Hard upon their heels came the vision of Jesus Christ truly present in the Holy Eucharist. This extraordinary favor was constant, given her every time she entered the chapel during the nine months of her novitiate; and there are certain indications that it may have continued from time to time during her entire life. The vision took a special form on Trinity Sunday, June 6, 1830, when Our Lord appeared to Catherine during Mass, robed as a king. At the reading of the Gospel the symbols of his kingship fell to the ground, and Catherine understood in her heart that the King of France, that stubborn old man, Charles X, would be overthrown. This vision of Christ the King has a peculiar fascination for the student of mystical phenomena, for its sole purpose seems to have been to foretell the fall of an earthly monarch.

But now, the great apparitions of Our Lady were at hand. Catherine has given us three complete accounts of them, written in her own hand at three distinct periods of her life. These accounts have such an indefinable charm, compounded of the accuracy of the eyewitness, the simplicity of the peasant, the eye for details of the woman, that it would be foolish not to let Catherine tell her marvelous story in her own words:

"On the eve of the feast of St. Vincent, good Mother Martha spoke to us of devotion to the saints, and to the Blessed Virgin in particular. It gave me so great a desire to see her that I went to bed with the thought that I would see my good Mother that very night—it was a desire I had long cherished.

"We had been given a piece of a surplice of St. Vincent's. I tore my piece in half, swallowed it, and fell asleep, confident that St. Vincent would obtain for me the grace of seeing the Blessed Virgin.

"At eleven-thirty, I heard someone calling my name:

" 'Sister, Sister, Sister!'

"Wide awake, I looked in the direction of the voice. Drawing the bed-curtains, I saw a child clothed in white, some four or five years old, who said to me:

" 'Come to the chapel; get up quickly and come to the chapel: the Blessed Virgin is waiting for you there.'

"At once the thought struck me: *Someone will hear me.*

"The child answered:

" 'Do not be afraid. It is eleven-thirty; everyone is asleep. Come, I am waiting for you.'

"He followed me, or rather I followed him;[1] he kept to my left, and was surrounded with rays of light. Wherever we went, the lights were lit, a fact which astonished me very much. But my surprise was greatest at the threshold of the chapel: the door opened of itself, the child scarcely having touched it with the tip of his finger. It was the height of everything, to see that all the torches and tapers were burning—it reminded me of midnight Mass. I did not see the Blessed Virgin. The child led me into the sanctuary, to the side of *M. le Directeur's* chair. There he remained the whole time.

"Since the time seemed long, I looked to see whether the watchers[2] were passing by the tribunes.

"Finally the hour came; the child announced it to me, saying:

" 'Here is the Blessed Virgin; here she is.'

"I heard a noise like the rustling of a silk dress, which came from the direction of the tribune near the picture of St. Joseph; a lady was seating herself in a chair on the altar steps at the Gospel side—just like St. Anne, only it was not the face of St. Anne.[3]

"I doubted whether it was the Blessed Virgin. Again the child, who stood by, the whole time, said to me:

" 'This is the Blessed Virgin.'

---

[1] Catherine seems to indicate here that, in her eagerness, she had started out ahead of her guide, then, remembering herself, fell back and let him take the lead.

[2] Sisters who remained on duty at night.

[3] Catherine is referring here to a picture of St. Anne seated in a chair, which hung in the sanctuary; Our Lady's attitude reminded her of this picture.

"It would be impossible for me to describe what I felt at that moment, or what passed within me, for it seemed to me that I did not look upon the Blessed Virgin.

"It was then that the child spoke, no longer as a child, but as a grown man, and in the strongest terms.[4]

"Looking upon the Blessed Virgin, I flung myself toward her, and falling upon my knees on the altar steps, I rested my hands in her lap.

"There a moment passed, the sweetest of my life. I could not say what I felt. The Blessed Virgin told me how I must conduct myself with my director, and added several things that I must not tell. As to what I should do in time of trouble, she pointed with her left hand to the foot of the altar, and told me to come there and to open up my heart, assuring me that I would receive all the consolation I needed.

"I asked her the meaning of everything I had seen, and she deigned to explain it to me.

"I could not say how long I stayed with her. When she left, it was as if she faded away, becoming a shadow which moved toward the tribune, the way she had come. I got up from the steps of the altar and saw that the child was where I had left him. He said:

" 'She is gone . . .'

"We went back the same way, always surrounded with light, the child still keeping to the left.

"I believe that this child was my guardian angel, who showed himself that he might take me to see the Blessed Virgin, for I had often prayed to him to obtain this favor for me. He was dressed in white, and shone with a mysterious light that was more resplendent than light itself; he appeared to be four or five years old.

---

[4] This is Catherine's way of expressing, as she has explained elsewhere, that the child suddenly assumed a man's voice and sternly admonished her for doubting that it was really the Blessed Virgin.

"Having returned to my bed, I heard two o'clock strike. I slept no more that night."

Catherine appended to this over-all account the actual words spoken by Our Lady during this interview. With her usual precision, she entitled it: *July Conversation with the Most Blessed Virgin, from 11:30 in the evening of the 18th until 1:30 in the morning of the 19th, St. Vincent's Day.*

"My child, the good God wishes to charge you with a mission. You will have much to suffer, but you will rise above these sufferings by reflecting that what you do is for the glory of God. You will know what the good God wants. You will be tormented until you have told him who is charged with directing you. You will be contradicted but, do not fear, you will have grace. Tell with confidence all that passes within you; tell it with simplicity. Have confidence. Do not be afraid.

"You will see certain things; give an account of what you see and hear. You will be inspired in your prayers: give an account of what I tell you and of what you will understand in your prayers.

"The times are very evil. Sorrows will befall France; the throne will be overturned. The whole world will be plunged into every kind of misery. (In saying this, the Blessed Virgin appeared very distressed.) But come to the foot of the altar. There graces will be shed upon all, great and small, who ask for them. Especially will graces be shed upon those who ask for them.

"My child, I particularly love to shed graces upon your Community; I love it very much. It pains me that there are great abuses in regularity, that the rules are not observed, that there is much relaxation in the two Communities.[5] Tell that to him who has charge of you, even though he is not the superior. He will be given charge of the Community in a special way; he

[5] The Vincentian Fathers form a Double Family with the Sisters of Charity; both have the same superior general. When Our Lady visited St. Catherine, the Communities of St. Vincent were passing through the painful days of reorganization that followed the French Revolution and the reign of Napoléon Bonaparte.

must do everything he can to restore the rule in vigor. Tell him for me to guard against useless reading, loss of time, and visits. When the rule will have been restored in vigor, a community will ask to be united to your Community. Such is not customary, but I love them; God will bless those who take them in; they will enjoy great peace.[6]

"The Community will enjoy a great peace; it will become large.[7] But, there will be an abundance of sorrows, and the danger will be great. Yet, do not be afraid; tell them not to be afraid. The protection of God will be ever present in a special way—and St. Vincent will protect you. (Now the Blessed Virgin was very sad.) I shall be with you myself. I always have my eye upon you. I will grant you many graces. The moment will come when the danger will be extreme. It will seem that all is lost. At that time, I will be with you. Have confidence. You will recognize my coming and the protection of God over the Community, the protection of St. Vincent over both Communities. Have confidence; do not be discouraged; I will be with you then.

"But it will not be the same for other communities—there will be victims (the Blessed Virgin had tears in her eyes when she said it)— among the clergy of Paris there will be victims—Monseigneur the Archbishop—(at this name the tears came afresh).

"My child, the cross will be treated with contempt; they will hurl it to the ground. Blood will flow; they will open up again the side of Our Lord. The streets will run with blood. Monseigneur the Archbishop will be stripped of his garments. (Here the Blessed Virgin could no longer speak; her anguish was depicted in her face.) My child, (she told me) the whole world will be in sadness. (At these words I wondered to myself when this would be, and I understood clearly, *forty years.*")

---

[6] Our Lady spoke of Mother Seton's Sisters from Emmitsburg, Maryland, who petitioned for union with St. Vincent's Community, and were admitted in 1849.

[7] Today it numbers 43,000 Sisters.

Like the apparitions of St. Vincent's heart, this apparition was a prelude to the great apparition of the Miraculous Medal on November 27. Catherine is to be entrusted with a mission, but she is not yet told what that mission will be. Our Lady does, however, foretell the dire happenings to befall France and the world in 1870, that year of turmoil and upheaval. There is some reason to believe that her predictions were not meant to apply only to the year 1870, for, during the revolution of 1830, which erupted just a week after this apparition, and during the revolution of 1848, these predictions were fulfilled at least in part. It is an especially striking fact that, although Archbishop Darboy was murdered in 1870, as Our Lady had foretold, so too, Archbishop Affré was shot to death on the barricades in 1848, and Archbishop de Quélen had twice to flee for his life during the "Glorious Three Days" of the revolution of 1830.

The fulfillment of these terrible prophecies of the Mother of God may be considered in a practical way as grim proof of the authenticity of the visions. They may be also looked upon as hints of even more horrible punishments to befall mankind, such as World Wars I and II, for which the "mission" to be entrusted to Catherine would be in the nature of a remedy.

There are several circumstances, immediately obvious, which distinguish this apparition from others. There is, first of all, what may be called its positiveness. There is never the slightest doubt that the lady of the apparition is the Blessed Virgin. Catherine had a momentary doubt, but this is perfectly natural and human in the circumstances, like the qualms of the Apostles concerning the reality of the Risen Christ. Objectively speaking, however, the lady is identified by the radiant child as the Blessed Virgin, even before her coming.

The second distinctive mark of the apparition is the intimacy of it. Catherine is admitted to a relationship with the Mother of God, is permitted to take liberties, granted to no other seer. To kneel with one's hands in Our Lady's lap and to chat with her for two hours is an unheard-of privilege. What is more, the privilege extended throughout Catherine's lifetime—not in this visible way, but in the depths of Catherine's soul. At Our Lady's last appearance to the saint, in January 1831,[8] the Virgin said: "You will see me no more, but you will often hear my voice in your prayers." There is positive proof that, throughout the remaining forty-six years of Catherine's life, this was so.

The apparition's third feature is the extreme volubility of the Mother of God. At no other time has this great Lady from heaven had so much to say to a child of earth. Catherine has reported *verbatim* but a fraction of the conversation; the actual interview consumed two whole hours.

At first glance there seems but one specific link with the apparitions of the next hundred years: the call to prayer. "Come to the foot of the altar." This apparition, however, cannot be considered alone; it is inevitably part of the apparition of the Miraculous Medal: an integral part—the beginning—of the series that stretches to Fatima and Banneux.

Catherine was left completely in the dark as to the nature of her mission. Four months were to pass before heaven revealed its plans to her. To give the revelation, again in Catherine's own words:

"On November 27, 1830, which fell upon the Saturday before the first Sunday of Advent, at five-thirty in the evening, in the deep silence after the point of the meditation had been read—that is, several minutes after the point of the meditation—I heard a sound like the rustling of a silk dress, from the tribune near the picture of St. Joseph. Turning in that direction, I saw the Blessed Virgin, at the level of St. Joseph's picture. The Virgin was standing. She was of medium height, and

---

[8] The apparition of the Miraculous Medal was repeated, probably five times in all, with very slight variations. The repetition was probably an urging to action in the striking of the Medal.

clothed all in white. Her dress was of the whiteness of the dawn, made in the style called "*à la Vierge*," that is, high neck and plain sleeves. A white veil covered her head and fell on either side to her feet. Under the veil her hair, in coils, was bound with a fillet ornamented with lace, about three centimeters in height or of two fingers' breadth, without pleats, and resting lightly on the hair. Her face was sufficiently exposed, indeed exposed very well, and so beautiful that it seems to me impossible to express her ravishing beauty.

"Her feet rested on a white globe, that is to say half a globe, or at least I saw only half. There was also a serpent, green in color with yellow spots.

"The hands were raised to the height of the stomach and held, in a very relaxed manner and as if offering it to God, a golden ball surmounted with a little golden cross, which represented the world. Her eyes were now raised to heaven, now lowered. Her face was of such beauty that I could not describe it.

"All at once I saw rings on her fingers, three rings to each finger, the largest one near the base of the finger, one of medium size in the middle, the smallest one at the tip. Each ring was set with gems, some more beautiful than others; the larger gems emitted greater rays and the smaller gems, smaller rays; the rays bursting from all sides flooded the base, so that I could no longer see the feet of the Blessed Virgin.

"At this moment, while I was contemplating her, the Blessed Virgin lowered her eyes and looked at me. I heard a voice speaking these words:

" 'This ball that you see represents the whole world, especially France, and each person in particular.'

"I could not express what I felt at this, what I saw, the beauty and the brilliance of the dazzling rays.

" 'They are the symbols of the graces I shed upon those who ask for them.'

"This made me realize how right it was to pray to the Blessed Virgin and how generous she was to those who did pray to her, what graces she gave to those who asked for them, what joy she had in giving them.

" 'The gems from which rays do not fall are the graces for which souls forget to ask,' (*continued the voice*).[9]

"At this moment, I was so overjoyed that I no longer knew where I was. A frame, slightly oval in shape, formed round the Blessed Virgin. Within it was written in letters of gold:

" 'O Mary, conceived without sin, pray for us who have recourse to thee.'

"The inscription, in a semi-circle, began at the height of the right hand, passed over the head, and finished at the height of the left hand.

"The golden ball disappeared in the brilliance of the sheaves of light bursting from all sides; the hands turned out and the arms were bent down under the weight of the treasures of grace obtained.

"Then the voice said:

" 'Have a Medal struck after this model. All who wear it will receive great graces; they should wear it around the neck. Graces will abound for those who wear it with confidence.'

"At this instant the tableau seemed to me to turn, and I beheld the reverse of the Medal: a large M surmounted by a bar and a cross; beneath the M were the Hearts of Jesus and Mary, the one crowned with thorns, the other pierced with a sword."

Within minutes after the vision had disappeared from her sight, "like a candle blown out," as Catherine put it, there began for the humble Sister the lifelong task of guarding her identity. Catherine understood from the Mother of God that, in giving the Medal to the world, she herself was to remain unknown. So completely caught up in the glorious experience was she that she had no recollection of leaving the

[9] This sentence is a supplement to the descriptive paragraph above concerning the rings, gems, and rays. Catherine does not mention in the former paragraph that some of the gems emitted no rays whatever.

chapel and going down to the refectory for supper; she was brought back to earth by the voice of the mistress of novices speaking in sarcasm:

"Sister Labouré must still be in ecstasy." She spoke more truly than she knew!

In the years that followed, Catherine Labouré became very adept at hiding her great secret, and the ways of community living were her greatest ally. Because of community routine she lived a life that was, on the surface, no different than the lives of the Sisters around her. Even while enjoying the most remarkable favors of heaven, she never missed a duty or an exercise of her religious rule. At times suspicion fastened upon her. There were many reasons why: Sister Séjole, without really knowing, was firmly convinced that Catherine was the Seer of the Medal and did not hesitate to say so; Catherine had been a novice in 1830 when Our Lady appeared; she had a great personal devotion to the Mother of God—all these, and the inconsequential reasons conjured up by the curious sometimes turned attention to Sister Catherine Labouré. But she was always able to turn aside the guesses and conjectures.

There can be little doubt that she received supernatural help in keeping her secret. This was especially evident when, in 1836, the Archbishop of Paris urged Catherine's confessor Father Aladel to have her come forward and testify in person at the first official inquiry into the origin of the Medal. After Catherine had repeatedly demurred, in evident trepidation and anguish, she finally came up with the astonishing statement that it would do no good for her to testify anyway, for she could remember no detail of the apparitions! That this was not pure invention on her part was proven by at least two more well-authenticated periods of forgetfulness at other intervals in her life.

After her days of glory Catherine spent the remaining forty-six years of her life in complete obscurity at the Hospice d'Enghien in the environs of Paris, first as cook, then as laundress and custodian of the clothes room, and finally, for forty years, in charge of the old men who were inmates of the house. It was a singularly humdrum life, without glamour, or even much of human gratitude. The ordinariness of it obscured even her heroic sanctity, so that none of Catherine's Sisters, except in hindsight, regarded her as more than a good and regular religious. There were certain moments when the glory shone through—as on the morning when her Sisters discovered her in ecstasy before a statue of the Virgin in the garden, or when she made some passing prediction that inevitably came true—but these were but momentary, and everyone quickly forgot them. Beneath the veneer of daily religious life, Catherine Labouré was deeply involved in the practice of heroic virtue, nay, more, she was in constant touch with heaven.

It was only in 1876, a scant six months before her death, that the secret greatness of Catherine was finally revealed. Our Lady had asked for the erection of a statue depicting her in the attitude of the first phase of the Apparition of November 27, as the "Virgin of the Globe," and the statue had not been made. Fearing to appear before Mary Immaculate without every last detail of her mission accomplished, Catherine broke her long silence in order that it might be done.

Father Aladel had died in 1865 and had been succeeded as Catherine's confessor by Father Chinchon. For reasons that can only be conjectured, neither of these men had seen to the making of the statue. Now Father Chinchon was suddenly missioned to a distant house, and Catherine, who knew supernaturally that she had but a few months to live, found herself bereft of her trusted confidant. In panic she rejected the idea of confiding in her new confessor, and went directly to the Superior General, to beg him to restore Father Chinchon as her confessor. Whether or not she meant to reveal herself to the General as the Sister of the Apparitions, we shall never know, for she grew confused in his presence and was able only to stammer her startling request. To the

General, therefore, she seemed to be just an old lady in her dotage. Gently but firmly he refused her request.

Catherine went home in tears. The Sister Superior gaped at her in astonishment, for she had never seen her upset before. When she asked Catherine what was the matter, Catherine suddenly grew calm and answered:

"Since I have not much longer to live, I feel that the time to speak out has come. But, as the Blessed Virgin told me to speak only to my confessor, I shall say nothing to you until I have asked Our Lady's permission in prayer. If she tells me I may speak to you, I will do so; otherwise I will remain silent."

The next morning, having secured the permission of the Mother of God, Catherine summoned her Superior, revealed herself as the Seer of the Apparitions, and begged that plans be set on foot for the making of the statue of the "Virgin of the Globe." Before her death she was to see the plaster model in the studio of the sculptor.

Catherine died peacefully on December 31, 1876. Pope Pius XI beatified her in 1933, and Pope Pius XII raised her to the honors of the altar in 1947. Her incorrupt body lies beneath an altar built on the spot where Our Lady appeared to her; above the altar is the statue, the making of which had caused her such anguish.

The great apparition of November 27, 1830, in which the Miraculous Medal was given to the world, must be considered under two broad aspects: first of all, theologically, and then, as a message to mankind.

The prominent theological doctrine of the apparition is, of course, the Immaculate Conception. The proper name of the Medal is the Medal of the Immaculate Conception, and it was so called from the beginning until the people themselves, pleased with the wonders it worked, called it the Miraculous Medal. The doctrine of the Immaculate Conception is symbolically portrayed in the representation of Mary crushing the head of the serpent, a reference to Genesis 3:15, "I will put enmities between thee and the woman, and thy seed and her seed; she shall crush thy head, and thou shalt lie in wait for her heel." The doctrine is specifically mentioned in the golden letters which formed round the Virgin: "O Mary, conceived without sin . . ."

There can be no doubt that the apparition of the Medal hastened the definition of the doctrine of the Immaculate Conception. It was indeed the "great sign" that "appeared in the heavens," an indication that the time was ripe for the vindication of Mary's glorious privilege. Pius IX himself asserted that the impetus for his pronouncement came from France. Archbishop de Quélen of Paris, who approved the making of the Medal and later confirmed the authenticity of the vision, had no small part in this impetus. In 1836 he dedicated his archdiocese to the Immaculate Conception, and it was through his urging that the title "Queen conceived without sin" was added to the Litany of Loreto. The apparition of the Medal, therefore, bears a significant relation to the apparitions at Lourdes. It is noteworthy that Bernadette was wearing a medallion that bore on its face the front of the Miraculous Medal when Our Lady appeared to her, and that she described the attitude of the Virgin, making a gracious, sweeping gesture with her arms, "just the way she appears on the Miraculous Medal."

The first phase of the apparition, popularly referred to as the "Virgin of the Globe," however, is concerned with the doctrine which describes Mary as the Mediatrix of all graces. Briefly, this doctrine, which is not yet defined by the Church but which is considered certain by theologians, states that all prayers and petitions, whether addressed specifically to Mary, or to God and the saints, are presented to God by her, and all graces, whether answers to prayer or gifts unsought, pass through her hands to mankind. This doctrine is admirably represented by the attitude of the Mother of God offering the golden ball which represents the world, to God, her lips moving in prayer—this is the intercessory office of Our Lady—and by the brilliant rays streaming from the rings on her hands, symbolic of the actual bestowal of the graces obtained.

This doctrine is also expressed in a general way in Our Lady's explanation of the dazzling rays: "They are the symbols of the graces *I shed* upon those *who ask for them.*"

In the second phase of the apparition this doctrine of the mediation of Mary continues to be expressed in the rays falling from the outstretched hands "bent down under the weight of the treasures of grace obtained," and the golden words: "O Mary, conceived without sin, *pray for us* who have recourse to thee."

On the back of the Medal there is obvious reference to Our Lady's part as Co-redemptress of the race in the Sacred Hearts of Jesus and Mary, "the one crowned with thorns, the other pierced with a sword," and in the M surmounted by a cross, which is plainly a representation of Mary beneath the Cross of her Son. Our Lady herself considered the back of the Medal to be readily understandable, for when Catherine, at the request of her confessor, Father Aladel, asked what words should be inscribed there, the Virgin replied: "The M and the two hearts express enough."

The twelve stars on the Medal, which Catherine does not mention in any written account of the vision, but which she described to her confessor by word of mouth, refer to the text from the Apocalypse, 12:1, "A woman clothed with the sun, and the moon under her feet, and on her head a crown of twelve stars."

The Medal received liturgical approbation when a Mass and Office were assigned in its honor at the direction of Aloisi Cardinal Masella, Prefect of the Sacred Congregation of Rites, in 1895. It is one of only three sacramentals in the history of the Church to be thus liturgically honored, sharing its distinction with the Rosary and the Brown Scapular.

As a message to mankind, the meaning of the Miraculous Medal apparition is thoroughly clear. The approach of Our Lady is personal to each human soul. She is concerned, not with mankind in general, but with each individual. "This ball represents the whole world, especially France, and *each person in particular.*" The Medal to be struck will be a personal link between Our Lady and each person who wears it. She does not call for pilgrimages, nor for the building of a shrine. This tiny Medal is to be her shrine, and her devotees are to carry it always about their necks. "Grace will abound for those who wear it with confidence."

It was and is the fulfillment of this promise, the abundance of graces, that quickly endeared the Medal to the world. The spread of the Medal was so rapid and the flood of favors it let loose so startling, that the faithful gave it the name "Miraculous." The number of Medals minted since 1832, when it was first struck, is beyond all counting. It is easily in the hundreds of millions. The Medal is worn by Protestant and Jew as well as Catholic.

The wonders it works are as ordinary or as extraordinary as the needs and ills of mankind. Conversions to the Faith, repentance of hardened sinners, recognition of the Will of God, peace in homes, recoveries from illness acute and chronic, critical and minor—the catalogue is endless. Each wearer of the Medal has his own story to tell. Best of all, the Medal seems to have a special power for promoting and deepening personal devotion to the Mother of God. Thus it has not merely a passing or momentary effect on the soul it touches, but an effect which is so lasting as to be, in many cases, eternal. Under this aspect, it has assumed a mighty role in the reconversion of the world, for it betters the individual soul, and the world's goodness is exactly equal to the sum of all good hearts.

Catherine Labouré is the perfect model of what Our Lady intended the Medal to do for mankind. As already stated, the Miraculous Medal is meant to sanctify those who wear it. Catherine Labouré is not a saint because she saw the Blessed Virgin, but because she cultivated devotion to her and allowed this devotion to influence her way of life. In so doing, she realized perfectly Our Lady's objective: not the performance of heroic, or even unusual, deeds by her clients, but the perfection of their ordinary states of life.

Catherine's formula was very simple: she did what she was supposed to do; she did it as well as she could; and she did it for God. It is a formula that everyone can, and should, follow. No one pretends that it is easy; the pursuit of virtue entails self-discipline and sacrifice: but it is attainable.

The sanctity of Catherine Labouré is proof. She is, therefore, the "Saint of Ordinary People," a flesh-and-blood rendering of the message of Mary to mankind through the Apparitions of the Miraculous Medal, a model for the salvation of the modern world.

SPECIAL NOTE

Mary Immaculate did not specifically ask for any set form of devotion beyond the wearing of the Medal. Yet, a great devotion of prayer to Our Lady of the Miraculous Medal has arisen as a sort of by-product. The chief form of this devotion is the Perpetual Novena in honor of Our Lady of the Miraculous Medal, which was established at Mary's Central Shrine, Germantown, Philadelphia, by Father Joseph A. Skelly, C.M., on Monday, December 8, 1930, and has continued there every Monday since. Yet more, the weekly novena is held in more than five thousand churches and chapels throughout the world, and is attended by more than 5,000,000 persons. In America a special band of fifty priests preaches this novena as its chief work. At the Central Shrine itself, between fifteen and twenty thousand people attend twelve services each Monday. It is especially notable that the novena has found its way from America to the Chapel of the Apparitions on the rue du Bac in Paris, and is quickly spreading throughout France.

LA SALETTE

1846

THE LADY
IN TEARS

Msgr. John S. Kennedy

The parish of La Salette in the diocese of Grenoble comprises a few tiny hamlets in the French Alps. Its setting is spectacular: a series of towering mountains, majestic and mysterious, thrusting at the sky, the peaks of some glittering with snow. One could not but be impressed by the grandeur here; no more could one fail to notice the loneliness. This is a place only skimpily populated, and far from the busy world. It has the quality of a natural sanctuary, somewhat removed, austere, silent.

It was the scene of an apparition of Our Lady to two rude cattle herders, Melanie Mathieu, aged 14, and Maximin Giraud, aged 11. This took place on Saturday afternoon, September 19, 1846.

The year is significant, right in the middle of the socially and politically turbulent nineteenth century. France was in ferment. The great Revolution was then much more recent than our own Civil War is today. It had been followed by the reign of Napoleon, with its further change and its constant warfare and its exactions of the people. Then defeat and a succession of shifts in government. Many ties with the traditional past had been violently sundered, much that was immemorial had been sent crashing to bits, and the situation in the country was uncertain.

Besides, in France and throughout the Western world, this was an age bristling with new ideas. Revolution was not confined to the political order; it affected all of life. Religion, for example, had suffered persecution or severe intellectual attack and was being countered by conceptions of man's nature and destiny radically different from those of Christianity. This had had impact even on the small, dull, isolated town of Corps, where Melanie's and Maximin's families lived.

Fewer and fewer went to Sunday Mass. The Sacraments were neglected. Once there had prevailed a Christian view of life, an awareness of God, a wholesome piety. Now there was far more cursing than praying, and Christian attitudes and observance had given way to self-indulgence, greediness, a hard worldly spirit.

We have said that Melanie and Maximin were natives of Corps. Curiously, although that town numbered hardly more than a thousand inhabitants, the pair had never met there. They first became acquainted in Ablandins, one of the hamlets in the parish of La Salette, on September 17, 1846. To Ablandins they had come as employees of two local farmers.

Their families were extremely poor. Melanie was one of eight children, and when she was still quite little she had been sent into the streets to beg. At seven she was hired out for whatever jobs she was capable of doing. Two or three years later she began to get seasonal work on farms. She was in Ablandins in 1846 as an employee of Baptiste Pra, whose small herd she daily took to and from pasturage high on the towering slopes.

She was a silent child, without gaiety. Withdrawn and timid, she was considered by some to be morose; life had been hard on her. She had had no schooling, had been infrequently to church, knew only a few scraps of the catechism which her mother had laboriously taught her, and could barely say the Lord's Prayer and the Hail Mary. But she was good at her work, performing it meticulously.

Maximin, by contrast, had spirit. He was reputed something of a scamp in Corps, where he spent much of his time aimlessly roaming the streets and playing games. The reason was that his was an unhappy home. His mother had died; his father had remarried; Maximin did not get on well with his stepmother. His father, a wheelwright, drank much of his earnings and was by turns sentimental and harsh. Like Melanie, Maximin was a stranger to school. He was brought to church occasionally, by his grandmother; and sometimes his father, in a fit of compunction, would spend a little time helping him to memorize the elementary prayers. More often Giraud would take the boy along to the café with him.

It was during one of these expeditions that Pierre Selme, from Ablandins, met the pair. Selme owned four cows which had to be brought to pasture in a mountain meadow adjoining that of Baptiste Pra. His herder was now ill; he required a temporary replacement. Giraud was prevailed upon to let Maximin take the job for a week. Maximin first met Melanie on Thursday, September 17. The following day they were in sight of each other in the fields, and on Saturday, at first light, started back for the mountain together.

At noon, as the Angelus sounded, the children drove the cows from the fields to a ravine, to water them at a spring called the fountain of the beasts. When this chore had been performed, Maximin and Melanie took from their knapsacks their lunches of bread and cheese, which they proceeded to eat with good appetite. Afterward they stretched out on the ground and napped.

Well over an hour later Melanie suddenly awoke, all solicitude for the cows. Where were they? Were they safe? She scrambled up, called to the sleeping boy, and the two ran to look for their charges. These, they soon saw, were placidly grazing.

It was getting on toward the middle of the afternoon; soon the journey down to Ablandins must be begun. Melanie turned back toward the ravine, to gather up the knapsacks and whatever scraps might be left from their meal. As she reached its lip, she suddenly halted, thunderstruck.

For below, in the ravine, she saw a large circle of brilliant light, vibrant and outshining the sun. After a moment she summoned enough voice to call to Maximin, "Come quickly! See the light down there!"

He dashed to her side. "Where?" he wanted to know. She pointed. He, too, saw it. As they watched, the splendor of the light intensified, dazzlingly. They were puzzled and fear-stricken and were about to flee when they observed that the luminous circle was opening. Gradually they could make out, ever more sharply defined, the figure of a woman. She was seated, her face in her hands, in an attitude of sorrow, weeping. Slowly, with unearthly grace, she arose. With her arms crossed on her breast and her head somewhat inclined, she confronted them.

The loveliness of her grieving face was magnetic. But they noticed as well the details of her vesture: the headdress topped by a lucent crown; the dress strewn with bursts of light; the slippers edged with roses; the golden crucifix hanging from a chain about her neck, a hammer on one side of it, a pair of pincers on the other. And all was suffused with glory.

As they gazed in fascination, the children heard the woman speak in a voice both commanding and reassuring. "Come to me, my children," she said. "Do not be afraid. I am here to tell you something of the greatest importance." She spoke in French, not in their patois. They found it hard to follow her, but grasped her meaning. They moved gingerly into the ravine, came within touching distance of her. They could now see her more closely and mark the crystalline tears upon her cheeks.

Again she addressed them, at first in French, later in their own dialect. "If my people will not obey, I shall be compelled to loose my Son's arm. It is so heavy, so pressing that I can no longer restrain it. How long I have suffered for you! If my Son is not to cast you off, I am obliged to entreat Him without ceasing. But you take no least notice of that. No matter how well you pray in future, no matter how well you act, you will never be able to make up to me what I have endured for your sake.

"I have appointed you six days for working. The seventh I have reserved for myself. And no one will give it to me. This it is which causes the weight of my Son's arm to be so crushing.

"The cart drivers cannot swear without bringing in my Son's name. These are the two things which make my Son's arm so burdensome.

"If the harvest is spoiled, it is your own fault. I warned you last year by means of the potatoes. You paid no heed. Quite the reverse, when you discovered that the potatoes had rotted, you swore, you abused my Son's name. They will continue to rot, and by Christmas this year there will be none left.

"If you have grain, it will do no good to sow it, for what you sow the beasts will devour, and any part of it that springs up will crumble into dust when you thresh it.

"A great famine is coming. But before that happens, the children under seven years of age will be seized with trembling and die in their parents' arms. The grownups will pay for their sins by hunger. The grapes will rot, and the walnuts will turn bad."

The woman continued speaking, turning toward Maximin. She was confiding a secret to him; Melanie could not hear a word of it. Then it was Melanie's turn to have a secret entrusted to her, and of this Maximin caught nothing.

The discourse audible to both resumed. "If people are converted, the rocks will become piles of wheat, and it will be found that the potatoes have sown themselves."

A pause, and then, with a searching look, "Do you say your prayers well, my children?"

"No," they murmured, shamefaced. "We say them hardly at all."

"Ah, my children, it is very important to say them, at night and in the morning. When you don't have time, at least say an Our Father and a Hail Mary. And when you can, say more."

Then a reversion to the theme of reproach. "Only a few rather old women go to Mass in the summer. All the rest work every Sunday throughout the summer. And in winter, when they don't know what to do with themselves, they go to Mass only to poke fun at religion. During Lent they flock to the butcher shops, like dogs."

Another question, "My children, haven't you ever seen spoiled grain?"

Maximin answered, "No, never."

"But my child, you must have seen it once, near Coin, with your papa. The owner of a field said to your papa, 'Come and see my spoiled grain.' The two of you went. You took two or three ears of grain in your fingers. You rubbed them, and they crumbled to dust. Then you came back from Coin. When you were but a half hour away from Corps, your papa gave you a piece of bread and said, 'Well, my son, eat some bread this year, anyhow. I don't know who'll be eating any next year, if the grain goes on spoiling like that.'"

She was right! Just such an incident had occurred; those very words had been spoken! Maximin had clean forgotten, but, astonishingly, this woman knew all about it. "It's very true, Madame," he muttered. "Now I remember it. Until now I did not."

The woman looked earnestly at them. "My children," she charged them, "you will make this known to all my people." Slowly she turned away, glided along the ravine, paused, and, without facing them, repeated the command, "You will make this known to all my people." She proceeded to higher ground. Melanie and Maximin followed.

She stood still a moment, then rose into the air. They saw her look toward heaven, joy in her face and her tears at an end. She glanced solicitously out over the world, southeast toward Rome. Her figure and the palpitant circle of light about it grew more resplendent, then began to disappear. She faded into the air.

The children stared at the spot where they had last seen her, and finally looked at each other. "Perhaps," said Melanie, "she was a great saint." It was the nearest either came to attributing any identity to the woman.

On their return to Ablandins, Maximin related the afternoon's experience to Selme, who was troubled by the story. After the evening meal he and the boy visited Pra's house and learned that Melanie had told her employer nothing of the curious happening. The girl was still busy with the stabling of the cattle, and before she came in Maximin repeated for the household the story of which he had informed Selme. When he had finished, Melanie was summoned. Questioned, she reluctantly gave her version of the occurrence. It tallied perfectly with Maximin's.

The silence following her grave recital was broken by Grandma Pra's saying to her son, "You see! You hear what the Blessed Virgin said to this child? I suppose you're still going to work tomorrow—it's Sunday, remember—after that!" These few words are notable in two respects: one, the old woman was the first to suggest that the lady of light was the Blessed Virgin; two, it was indeed habitual, as the lady had complained, that people worked on Sunday as if it were a weekday and not sacred to the Lord.

The next morning, very early, the children were sent off to the priest's house at La Salette to confide to the pastor what they had seen and heard. He immediately told them, "It must have been the Blessed

Virgin whom you saw." A little afterward, at Mass, he gave the congregation a highly emotional account of the children's experience. He observed none of the reserve and caution with which the Church regards such reports. This fact was noted with distress by Peytard, the mayor, a good, hardheaded man who feared a hoax or a prank on the children's part.

Later in the day Maximin went back to Corps, his period of service completed. Selme accompanied the boy, who, not finding his father at home, set out for his grandmother's, where he repeated his story. Meanwhile Selme had traced Giraud to the drinkshop, reported Maximin's safe return, and informed Giraud of what the children said they had witnessed. The town was soon buzzing with excitement; everyone was talking of the purported wonder.

In Ablandins, Mayor Peytard visited the Pra home. Melanie was required to tell him what she had disclosed the night before. She did so. He cross-questioned her. She could not be trapped. He threatened her with jail. She did not flinch. He ridiculed her. She would not budge. He offered her money if she would forget her story. She refused it. He left, thwarted and, against his will, impressed.

That night Pra invited to his house Selme and Jean Moussier, a town councilor. Once more Melanie was obliged to give an account of the experience she had shared with Maximin. Once more she did so without variation. This time Pra got it all down in writing, a most important step, taken some thirty hours after the alleged event.

Within the next eight days the children were twice conducted back to the scene of that event. The following Sunday they were brought there by Peytard, who asked the sergeant of police at Corps to come along. On the mountain the children re-enacted their experience, going through it step by step, in a way altogether unhesitant and according perfectly with the accounts they had given. Peytard was the more impressed. The policeman resorted to bluff. He accused Melanie and

Maximin of lying and shouted that he would lock them up. They did not falter.

The very next day they had to make the long, laborious trip all over again at the order, and in the company, of the parish priest of Corps, M. Mélin. M. Mélin had held himself aloof from the excitement in Corps. He was determined that this business should be critically sifted. He had once served at the cathedral in Grenoble, was well acquainted with the bishop, and knew that the bishop would sternly disapprove any least sign of ecclesiastical approbation until the matter had been slowly and exhaustively investigated and a firm favorable conclusion reached.

Accordingly, their pastor had summoned the children to his house when he learned that Melanie was in Corps for a brief visit to her family. He put them in separate rooms, listened first to one, then to the other, then brought them together for a rigorous grilling. He could not confound them and could find no inconsistencies in what they said. He had thereupon directed them to go to the mountain with him and five other persons who could be trusted to scrutinize everything with an acute, impartial eye.

At the ravine the children again reconstructed their experience, moving unstudiedly from spot to spot, describing what had happened, repeating the words said to them and the few words they had said. Again, no differences from their previous accounts, no inconsistencies. At the close of an interrogation by the six adults, someone suggested that the party kneel and say the Rosary. The priest did not object. In fact, he led the prayers.

When it came time to leave, one of the men proposed to break off a piece of the rock on which the lady of light had sat. He found that a spring was gushing out beside it. This had been a water source, but only after heavy rains or when the snows were melting. Now, with neither having occurred, the spring flowed steadily and copiously. Water from it was brought back to town in a bottle. It was given to a woman who had long been seriously ill. She began a novena to Our Lady, and each day of it she drank a little of the water. On the ninth day she quit her bed and resumed her normal life, her health perfectly restored.

M. Mélin composed a letter to Bishop de Bruillard. He told of the intensive, repeated interrogation of the children. "Neither threats nor promises availed in getting them to change their story," he said. "They always say the very same thing and to whoever wants to listen to them. I have gone very deliberately into every bit of information which I could lay hands on. I have found nothing which suggests in the remotest way either trickery or lying . . . It is the view of the people, naturally, that the Mother of God has come to warn the world before her Son rains down punishments. My own conviction, in the light of all the evidence I have been able to gather, is identical with the people's, and I believe that this warning is a great favor from heaven."

The bishop, shortly thereafter, sent to all the priests of his diocese a stern reminder that it was up to him, and him alone, to judge the supposed happening. "We have in no way pronounced on the event in question," he declared. "Wisdom and duty require of you, therefore, the greatest reserve and, above all, a complete silence on this subject in the pulpit."

In order to get the preliminaries of an official Church inquiry under way, Bishop de Bruillard sent to La Salette, in October, Father Chambon, superior of the Grenoble minor seminary, and three others of its faculty, to make an investigation. In November he had their report and, after studying it, appointed two commissions of his most learned priests, charging each group to examine, independently of the other, the Chambon findings, as well as the quantity of documents concerning the reported apparition which had been accumulating at the bishop's house.

Meanwhile, quite spontaneously, pilgrimages to La Salette had begun, first from the nearby towns, then from a much wider area. People toiled up the mountain in great numbers, prayed at the ravine, drew water from the spring. The priests did not interfere; no more did they participate. More miraculous cures were reported.

What M. Mélin observed with particular satisfaction was that, in Corps, the remonstrances and pleas of the lady of light were having an effect. Violation of the Sunday rest ceased to be the common practice. Regularly present now at Mass were people who had been missing it for years. Long lines waited before the confessional, and the communion rail was unaccustomedly thronged. Holidays which once had been religious in nature and observance, but in late years had been no more than occasions for scandalous drinking and carousing, reacquired their original character. His fellow priests in the parishes of the region reported a similar change in their charges.

Naturally there was great curiosity about Melanie and Maximin, and the bishop thought it best, for their protection, that they should enter the school of the Sisters of Providence in Corps. Melanie was to board there, Maximin to come in by the day. The nuns would instruct them in religion, prepare them for first Communion (past due for each), and shelter them from the importunate and the sensation-seeking.

But this sanctuary did not save them from further quizzing. Arduous though the experience was for the children, it served to confirm their absolute fidelity to the account they had given on the very day of their great experience.

Thus, Father Lagier, a native of Corps, returned there in the winter of 1846–47 to be at the bedside of his dying father. As the patient lingered, the priest used his leisure to interview the children. He questioned Melanie for no fewer than fifteen hours, and his examination was sharp, not to say merciless. He dragged her over the same ground again and again. He arrowed trickily worded queries at her. He thunderingly demanded she disclose the secret she maintained had been entrusted to her. But whatever device he resorted to, he could not rattle her or involve her in contradictions. No more could he discompose Maximin.

There were other inquiries, one on orders from the government in Paris. The La Salette story had by now been featured in papers all over France, and the secularist and anti-religious journals had had a field day with it, distorting facts, inventing maliciously, and pouring out scathing mockery. The Royal Prosecutor at Grenoble was directed to look into the "pretended apparition" and to punish its "inventors." Accordingly, there was a six-hour session in Corps, comprising a deluge of questions interspersed with frequent threats of stringent penalties. The result was a report which, after detailing the children's answers, said, "This statement does not differ from what they told their employers when they got home on the evening of the day of the apparition."

Still, the Minister of Justice and of Cults peremptorily lectured Bishop de Bruillard, "It is important, you will understand, to stop this evil thing in its tracks by telling the people the truth, and to thwart the blameworthy maneuvers the success of which is the easier in that they make an appeal to religious sentiment." The bishop replied blandly, promising nothing.

With the coming of spring, 1847, the pilgrimages, which the fierce winter weather in the mountains had stopped, resumed. Interest had not died out, as some had predicted. Now the crowds were larger than ever and included people from great distances indeed. La Salette became what it was to remain, a center of fervent prayer.

In July, Bishop de Bruillard instituted a formal juridical inquiry into the reputed apparition. This the two commissions which he had put to work the previous autumn had recommended. Heading the inquiry were Father Rousselot, a professor of theology at the major seminary, and Father Orcel, superior of that seminary. These were authorized to consult all clergy and laymen who might aid in the investigation, and especially any doctors who had treated people said to have been cured after invocation of Our Lady under the title of La Salette or after drinking water from the reportedly miraculous spring.

The inquiry lasted for many months. It involved visits to nine dioceses in which cures in some way associated with La Salette were said to have occurred. Half a dozen bishops were consulted. Once again the children were interrogated; once again they were brought to the mountain. Their travels done, Fathers Rousselot and Orcel returned to Grenoble.

The days leading up to the anniversary of the children's experience, September 19, 1847, saw thousands of pilgrims already overflowing all accommodations in the mountain hamlets and the towns in the vicinity. By the eve of the anniversary, newcomers could find no shelter and had to spend the night in the open. Before dawn on the morning of the nineteenth, Masses began to be celebrated at improvised altars at the scene of the alleged apparition. They went on almost until noon, attended by tens of thousands, with many receiving Holy Communion. It was estimated that between fifty and sixty thousand people were on the mountain during that day, praying and waiting in line to draw water from the spring; this was evidence of the extent and the depth of the popular devotion which had developed.

In the following month the priests entrusted with the juridical inquiry made their report to the bishop. They said that the consistency of the children's story was altogether extraordinary, the more so when one realized how astute some of their interrogators had been: men experienced in sizing up witnesses, in assessing evidence, in cross-questioning. It was unthinkable that the children had concocted the story; they were incapable of any such invention. Nor had they been coached by someone else; the closest investigation had turned up no hint of anything of the sort.

Striking, said the report, was the acceptance of the story by the people of Ablandins and La Salette. Their acceptance had been far from quick. At first they had been skeptical, had scoffed. Their assent had been hard-won and was now impervious to challenge.

Attention was called to twenty-three claimed cures. Stressed, too, was the conversion to consistent Christian living both in the diocese and beyond, which was directly attributable to the message which had now been widely spread.

The bishop's delegates affirmed their own acceptance of "the extraordinary event of La Salette." But he sought further opinions. He named a board of sixteen priests, outstanding for their perspicacity, piety, and erudition, to discuss the delegates' report. This board held eight meetings, at weekly intervals, in the bishop's presence, and freely fine-combed the report. The bishop listened and in mid-December concluded the sessions without comment. He made no pronouncement for four years. In the interval many significant things happened.

At Corps, for example, the Sisters of Providence had plenty of opportunity to observe Melanie and Maximin. They noticed that the children were not naturally compatible. Markedly different in disposition, they were often at odds with each other. In fact, about all that they agreed upon was what had happened to them on the mountain. That in this, and this alone, they were indefectibly at one, certainly strengthened the credibility of their claim.

They were not saints, and they knew it. But they did not delight in the notoriety which they had achieved. They insisted that attention should not be directed to them, but to the reputed apparition. When people pressed money on them, they abruptly refused it. A pilgrim who asked Melanie to touch a child suffering from some speech defect, and so cure it, was indignantly repulsed by the girl.

In 1850 there occurred an event which, for a while, put La Salette under a cloud. Some men interested in Maximin thought that he had a vocation to be a Marist religious. They proposed to take him to Ars, so that the celebrated curé there, Jean Baptiste Vianney, might advise him. Maximin agreed to go.

The Curé d'Ars believed the apparition authentic, had a picture of

Our Lady of La Salette in his house, and blessed religious articles bearing representatives of the children's experience. But when Maximin came to Ars, he was first received by the curé's brusque and combative assistant, who summarily accused him of being a liar. After listening to considerable railing, Maximin replied, "You'll have it your way. If you suppose that I actually saw nothing, then you'll call me a liar." The assistant informed M. Vianney that the lad had, in effect, admitted being a liar.

The next morning Maximin briefly met the curé, who asked whether he had seen the Blessed Virgin. Maximin said that he had seen a beautiful lady, but did not know whether or not she was the Blessed Virgin. He was, of course, right, since it was for the Church, and not for him, to pronounce on the lady's identity. But the curé seemed disturbed and went on to inquire whether Maximin had ever told lies. The boy admitted that he had, meaning lies of excuse. The curé apparently concluded that Maximin was repudiating the apparition as fraudulent.

For some time thereafter M. Vianney gave up his devotion to Our Lady of La Salette, and this was taken as a sure sign that the apparition had been discredited. But the curé's abandonment of credence in La Salette caused him intense pain. He was constantly disquieted about it. Some years later he said that he determined to put the matter to a test by asking an important favor of Our Lady under the title of La Salette. It was instantly granted. "I am a firm believer in La Salette," he said. "I have been represented as not believing in it. On the contrary, I am a firm believer in it. That boy and I did not understand each other. But I have asked heaven for signs to bolster my faith, and I have had them."

Another development was the decision to ask the children to write out the secrets entrusted to them, so that these might be transmitted to the Pope. This was prompted by pressure, brought by at least one highly placed churchman, for revelation of the secrets to him. Melanie and Maximin were reluctant to comply, but when the Holy Father's authority was explained to them, they gave their consent.

What they wrote was seen by no one save Pope Pius IX, to whom the two sealed envelopes were carried by Father Rousselot and Father Gerin in 1851. Father Rousselot stayed on in Rome for some time, was pleased by the evidence of acceptance of La Salette which he found among cardinals and bishops, and was gratified above all to be told by His Holiness that Bishop de Bruillard should go ahead and make such pronouncement on the apparition as the carefully considered facts justified.

Bishop de Bruillard proceeded to draw up the document, enlisting the collaboration of his friend, Bishop Villecourt of La Rochelle, who was destined to be a cardinal. After its completion it was sent to Rome, to be examined by Cardinal Lambruschini, who approved it on the condition that a single minor alteration be made. On November 16, 1851, it was read to the congregation at every Mass in the diocese.

"Five years ago," it began, "we were told of an event most extraordinary and, at first hearing, unbelievable, as having occurred on a mountain in our diocese. It was a matter of nothing less than an apparition of the Blessed Virgin, who was said to have been seen by two herders on September 19, 1846. She told them of evils threatening her people, especially because of blasphemy and the profanation of Sunday, and she confided to each a particular secret, forbidding that these be communicated to anyone.

"In spite of the natural candor of the two herders; in spite of the impossibility of collusion by two ignorant children who hardly knew each other; in spite of the constancy and firmness of their witness, which has never varied either when confronted by the agents of the law or by thousands of persons who have exhausted every trick to involve them in contradictions or wrest their secrets from them, it has been our duty to refrain for a long time from accepting an event which seemed to us marvelous.

"Haste on our part would not only have been contrary to the prudence which the great Apostle recommends to a bishop; it would also have served to buttress the prejudices of the enemies of our religion and of a great many Catholics who are Catholics in name only. While a multitude of pious souls warmly welcomed this reputed apparition as a fact, we again and again considered with care all the grounds which could lead us to reject it. Hence we have braved until now the criticisms which we well know have been directed at us by people who, with the best of intentions in other respects, accuse us, perhaps, of indifference or even of stark lack of faith.

"On the other hand, we were strictly obliged not to regard as impossible an event which the Lord (who would dare deny it?) might well have permitted to further His glory, for His arm is not shortened and His power is the same today as in ages past.

"While our episcopal duty imposed on us the necessity of waiting, pondering, fervently begging the light of the Holy Spirit, the number of wonders noised about on all sides was constantly growing. There was word of unusual cures worked in different parts of France and in other places, even countries far away. Sick people in desperate straits, either given up by their doctors as certain to die soon or condemned to long drawn out suffering, have been reported restored to perfect health after invocation of Our Lady of La Salette and the use, with faith, of the water from the spring at which the Queen of Heaven appeared to the two herders.

"From the very first days, people have spoken to us of this spring. We have been assured that it had never before flowed steadily, but gave water only after snow or heavy rains. It was dry that September 19; thereafter it began to flow and has flowed constantly ever since: marvelous water, if not in its origin, at least in its effects."

After outlining the extended process of investigation and instancing his consultation with other bishops, Bishop de Bruillard made his formal declaration, which reads in part:

"Considering, in the first place, the impossibility of explaining the fact of La Salette in any other way than by divine intervention, whether it is looked at in itself, in its circumstances, or in its essentially religious aim;

"Considering, in the second place, that the marvelous consequences of the fact of La Salette are the witness of God Himself, manifesting Himself by miracles, and that this witness is superior to that of men and their objections;

"Considering that these two grounds, taken separately or, much the more, together, ought to dominate the whole question and deprive of every trace of validity those contrary pretensions or suppositions of which we declare that we are fully aware;

"Considering, finally, that obedience and submission to Heaven's warnings can spare us the new chastisements with which we are threatened, while too long resistance can lay us open to evils beyond repair;

"On the express demand of all the members of our venerable chapter of canons and of the overwhelming majority of the priests of our diocese;

"Having invoked afresh the Holy Spirit and the assistance of the Immaculate Virgin;

"We declare the following:

"1. We give judgment that the apparition of the Blessed Virgin to two herders on September 19, 1846, on the mountain of the Alpine chain situated in the parish of La Salette, in the territory of the archpriest of Corps, bears in itself all the marks of truth, and the faithful have grounds to believe it indubitable and certain.

"2. We believe that this event acquires a further degree of certitude from the immense and spontaneous flocking of the faithful to the scene of the apparition, as well as from the abundance of marvels which have come in the wake of this event and a very great number of which cannot be called in doubt without violating the rules of human testimony.

"3. Therefore, to demonstrate our lively thanks to God and to the glorious Virgin Mary, we authorize the cult of Our Lady of La Salette."

In May of the following year, Bishop de Bruillard, though now aged, made the ascent of the mountain at La Salette to lay the cornerstone of the basilica which he was having built at the scene of the apparition. At about the same time, at his direction, a new community of priests began functioning there, called the Missionaries of La Salette. This was to grow and to establish houses in many parts of the world.

The shrine of Our Lady of La Salette became ever more popular as a place of pilgrimage, drawing many thousands annually, a good proportion of these from outside France. The number of miraculous cures attributed to the intercession of its patroness grew steadily.

However, most impressive was the spiritual influence at work at the shrine. The devout, of course, wanted to go to confession during their visits. But hardened sinners as well, people who had not been to the Sacraments for decades, people who had long since ceased to practice their religion and had even become scoffers at it, experienced in the place where Our Lady had pleaded for penitence, an overmastering pull toward the Sacrament of Penance.

There is on record the witness of many a man, rigid in indifference, who, on coming to La Salette out of curiosity, was surprised to experience recognition of his wretched state of soul, a realization of his sins and their enormity, compunction for them, a desire for release from them, the inviting prospect of a new and different life. La Salette was seen to be as a mighty font of extraordinary graces, and Our Lady of La Salette was hailed by the title "Reconciler of Sinners."

In 1879 the basilica, completed at last, was consecrated, and the Cardinal Archbishop of Paris, acting as the delegate of the Holy Father, crowned the statue representing Mary as she had appeared more than thirty years before to the two herders.

Neither was at hand for this double ceremony. Maximin had died in

1875, and Melanie was far away. Some people have considered that their careers, after the great event of 1846, cast doubt upon it. This is a completely false assumption.

Maximin, restless and incapable of concentration as in childhood, tried to prepare for the priesthood, found he had no vocation, began on a number of lines of work which came to nothing for him, died at forty.

Melanie, subjected to so much attention and shown exaggerated deference by the laity and even some of the clergy, eventually came to crave both. She made several attempts to enter the religious life, but never could accept the obscurity and the discipline which this imposed. She became a wanderer, seeking notice, giving highly colored accounts of her childhood in order to attract notice, and uttering threats especially against the clergy and the religious because of their failure to perceive and proclaim her personal importance. She died in 1904 while dressing to go out to Mass, at which she assisted daily.

In these lives there is nothing which impugns the authenticity of the apparition. To their dying breath neither Melanie nor Maximin retracted or changed the least particular of their common account of it. Their inconstancy in so much else makes all the more remarkable their constancy in this.

Again, in these lives there are failure and foolishness, but nothing bad. The two did not become saints; but they were always devoted Catholics. Evidently, they did not have the call to heroic sanctity, as, for example, Bernadette did. Their role, rather, was to be witnesses, and they fulfilled it unexceptionably. That is precisely the point about them, and it should never be let out of focus.

The message which they were selected to transmit, and which they faithfully did transmit, is the now familiar one. Twelve years after the apparition at La Salette the same message was reiterated at Lourdes. In our own century it has been sounded once more at Fatima. It is an indictment of man's disobedience to God, of man's forgetfulness of God, of a whole society's drift away from the life of faith and love to one of worldliness.

At La Salette, Our Lady instanced abuses common in the district where Melanie and Maximin lived, abuses indicative of a turning away from religion: the serving of self rather than of God, gross irreverence toward Him and disregard for His law, the discontinuance of prayer, spurning of the Mass, contemptuous neglect of the Sacraments, an attitude of mockery toward all that is sacred.

Was all this peculiar to the district? Certainly and sadly not. The condition was generally the same across the world. Disbelief, irreligion, withdrawal from God and His Church were common. Carelessness and lukewarmness had replaced concern for religion and loving practice of it. The minds of men paid scant heed to God, their hearts had no room for Him, and in their aspirations and plans He did not figure. They were sure they were building a better world, and insuring a brighter future, without Him. They were in error, as the event has proved.

Our Lady came to warn and to plead. She came to call men back, to stir up their faith, to induce them to pray and do penance. Only by prayer and penance can mankind's descent to calamity be averted. The offense of our kind is rank. Propitiation for it is possible only in Christ the Saviour, His Mother and ours reminds us. In Him must we live; with Him and through Him must we pray and make sacrifice. Unless we do, divine chastisement cannot be warded off. Mary calls to us: we must attend to her words and act upon them.

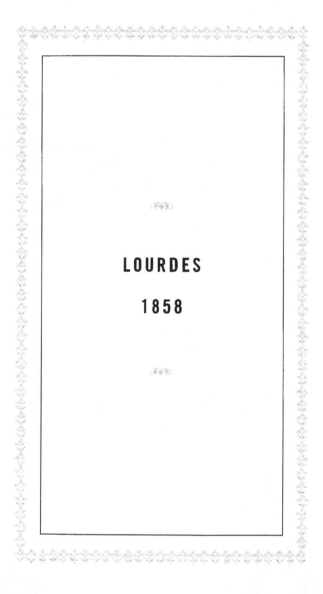

LOURDES

1858

BERNADETTE AND
THE BEAUTIFUL LADY

Frances Parkinson Keyes

"Few indeed are those who . . . are present as
eyewitnesses of one of those rare but terribly
real occurrences in which the omnipotence of
God strikes through the shadows of time and
space to bind up and heal the broken bodies
of men. But the evidence of these visitations
is indisputable. During the last century it has
pleased God so to visit His people time after
time at a remote grotto in the French
foothills of the Pyrénées, where the Blessed
Virgin Mother of God appeared in 1858 to
little Bernadette Soubirous. God of course
chooses His own times and places and occasions for the miraculous, but His power
shines forth most frequently where His
Mother is honored and venerated."

The above quotation was taken from an
important editorial which appeared in the

Catholic weekly *America*, for January 1958. It is important to us, in the present study of a certain saint, for two reasons: it singles out Bernadette Soubirous—a young Bigourdane peasant of sordid background, elementary education, and limited opportunity—as a striking example of the many "lowly and meek" exalted by the Almighty for one of those "rare examples" of occurrences when the omnipotence of God strikes through the shadows of time and space; and it stresses the point that, whereas God chooses His Own times and places and occasions for such miracles, "His power shines forth most frequently where His Mother is honored and venerated."

There is another important point which might be stressed in the same connection: when Bernadette first went to the grotto of Massabieille, which has now become world famous, it was without the slightest inkling that anything extraordinary, much less miraculous, was about to happen. She went because she and all her family, including her little brothers and sisters, were cold and hungry, and there was nothing in the hovel where they lived which would supply fuel for warmth and cooking; and the trip was one which involved hardship and even some danger. Her reward for persisting in this hazardous undertaking was overwhelming, not only to her personally, but to the whole world.

There is a story—it may be merely a legend, but never mind, its lesson is nonetheless poignant—of a mystic who was enjoying a rarely sublime vision when the cloister bell rang, summoning all the monks of the community to Vespers. He heard it clearly, despite his state of abstraction, but he hesitated: if his vision were interrupted, how would he ever be able to recapture it? And yet, he was bound by his vows of obedience to observe the rules of his monastery. Reluctantly, but still persuaded he was doing the right thing, he went to the chapel. When Vespers were over, he returned to the scene of his vision and lo! he was able to resume it at exactly the point where he had broken away from it. And, as it continued, he found he had become not only clairvoyant, but clairaudient; distinctly, he heard a Divine Voice say, "If you had not done your manifest duty, your vision would have vanished and you would never have known its culmination. What is more, you would never have had another."

I have often thought of this story in connection with Bernadette; if she had not gone to the grotto to gather firewood, which was her manifest duty, she would never have seen the Beautiful Lady who transfigured her life and who, through her, has transfigured the lives of millions in the century just past.

Her existence up to then, far from being tinged with glory, had been, for the most part, pitifully barren. Her parents, François and Louise Soubirous, were not unprincipled, as they have often been pictured, but they were improvident—a rare trait among French peasants. Their mill, of which their living quarters were an integral part, was forfeited for debt; they could find no better shelter than one small dark room, at the rear of a miserable little building called the *cachot*, which had once served as a jail and the front part of which a stonemason used as a workshop. Largely because it seemed literally impossible for the family to have its entire being in such cramped quarters, Bernadette, the eldest child, was sent to Bartrès, a nearby village, to live with some people named Avarant, who employed her as a shepherdess. Though harshly treated in the Avarant household, her long days in the field were not only contented but rewarding, as they have been to so many others similarly placed, from the time of David until the present; while, in her case, they did not bring forth sweet songs, they did result in habits of contemplation and prayer, and made her visualize her Divine Saviour from the beginning, not as a dim and distant figure, but as the Good Shepherd Who watched over His flock, to the last stray lamb, with tenderness and compassion. She was conscious of His Presence in the fragrant fields, surrounded by beautiful mountains, where she minded her patrons' sheep; and she needed no human companionship to make her happy.

But, for some reason which has never been adequately explained, though she had been taught her catechism by Mère Avarant, no provision had been made at Bartrès for her First Holy Communion; she asked for permission to return to Lourdes, in order to join the class at the Hospice which was being prepared for this.

The Hospice provided a shelter for some twenty or thirty impoverished old people, but its primary purpose, at that time, was educational in character. It was directed—as it still is—by the Sisters of Charity and Christian Education, whose Mother House was—as it still is—in Nevers. At Lourdes it took charge of some five hundred pupils, divided into three groups, of which the largest—the one to which Bernadette belonged—was made up of poor children whose parents could not afford to pay anything for even the rudiments of an education. (The other two groups, comprising both day pupils and boarders, were girls in more comfortable circumstances and of more cultured background; their courses took them beyond elementary grades.) Six months elapsed between the time Bernadette entered the Hospice and the time she made her First Holy Communion, which took place on the third of June, 1848. She did not have a good head for figures, and, at school, she did not seem to have a very retentive memory, though, eventually, this was to seem remarkable elsewhere; and during this brief period she learned to read with ease and to write in a singularly clear and delicate hand. She also showed a great aptitude for fine sewing or, indeed, any task which required the skillful use of her fingers; and these became more and more deft as she grew older. She carried a little basket which contained not only the black bread that constituted her *goûter*, but the stockings she was perpetually knitting, as she went back and forth between the *cachot* and the Hospice every day. She was not exactly pretty, but she was attractive; her skin was clear and rosy, and the softness of her large dark eyes was frequently enlivened by a sparkle. She had a pleasant smile, a rich voice, and a sense of humor which was lively, but untinged with malice. It comes as no surprise to learn that she was extremely popular with her schoolmates and that her teachers thought well of her. But she did not seem in the least remarkable to either group. She was just one more young girl, small for her age, which was fourteen, though she seemed much younger, who romped at recess, folded her hands quietly when she sat down, and did not always seem to pay strict attention during catechism classes. It is probable that she received more enlightenment than was apparent in regard to the Sacraments; and, when the great day came, she looked very lovely in the long white dress and flowing veil which is the traditional wear, throughout Latin countries, for little girls when they make their First Holy Communion. As a usual thing, she steadfastly declined any gift, whether of food or clothing, which could be interpreted as representing charity. But, on this occasion, she gratefully accepted the beautiful raiment offered her by a generous benefactor; none of her companions was more exquisitely attired.

When she was not at school, she made herself generally helpful to her mother, through her care of the younger children and her willingness to run errands, but especially to glean. Stray branches often fell from the trees which bordered the River Gave that flows through Lourdes, and she gathered these systematically. At a point where the river and an old canal met, there was a dark, rocky grotto, covered with clumps of bushes, from which twigs also sometimes fell. But, though there was an ancient saying that someday "a great wonder would be wrought at Massabieille," the place was very generally looked upon with disfavor. Sometimes fishermen took refuge there in a storm and sometimes, under the same circumstances, shepherds sought it out as protection for their sheep. It therefore seems especially appropriate that it should have been the scene of "great wonder" for a girl who was essentially a shepherdess, and who had doubtless heard other tenders of flocks speak of it as a shelter. But there is nothing to indicate that on her first visit to it which made history, there was any such thought of it in her mind. All sorts of interpretations have been put on this visit, and

I have consistently thought it best to let her tell her experience in her own words, which she did again and again, without variation, in speaking to the man who became one of her greatest friends—J. B. Estrade, a minor government official, who faithfully recorded her words.

"The Thursday before Ash Wednesday[1] it was cold and the weather was threatening. After our dinner my mother told us that there was no more wood in the house and she was vexed. My sister Toinette[2] and I, to please her, offered to go and pick up dry branches by the riverside. My mother said 'no' because the weather was bad and we might be in danger of falling into the Gave. Jeanne Abadie, our neighbor and friend, who was looking after her little brother in our house and who wanted to come with us, took her brother back to his house and returned the next moment telling us that she had leave to come with us. My mother still hesitated, but seeing that there were three of us she let us go. We took first of all the road which leads to the cemetery, by the side of which wood is unloaded and where shavings can sometimes be found. That day we found nothing there. We came down by the side which leads near the Gave and, having arrived at Pont Vieux, we wondered if it would be best to go up or down the river. We decided to go down and, taking the forest road, we arrived at Merlasse. There we went into Monsieur de la Fitte's field by the mill of Savy. As soon as we had reached the end of this field, nearly opposite the grotto of Massabieille, we were stopped by the canal of the mill we had just passed. The current of this canal was not strong for the mill was not working, but the water was cold and I for my part was afraid to go in. Jeanne Abadie and my sister, less timid than I, took their sabots in their hand and crossed the stream. However, when they were on the other side, they called out that it was cold and bent down to rub their feet and warm

---

[1] This was February 11, 1858.

[2] Bernadette's sister's name was Toinette Marie but she was often referred to simply as Toinette or Marie.

them. All this increased my fear, and I thought that if I went into the water I should get an attack of asthma. So I asked Jeanne Abadie, who was bigger and stronger than I, to take me on her shoulders.

" 'I should think not,' answered Jeanne; 'you're a mollycoddle; if you won't come, stay where you are.'

"After the others had picked up some pieces of wood under the grotto they disappeared along the Gave. When I was alone I threw stones into the bed of the river to give me a foothold, but it was of no use. So I had to make up my mind to take off my sabots and cross the canal as Jeanne and my sister had done.

"I had just begun to take off my first stocking when suddenly I heard a great noise like the sound of a storm. I looked to the right, to the left, under the trees of the river, but nothing moved; I thought I was mistaken. I went on taking off my shoes and stockings; then I heard a fresh noise like the first. I was frightened and stood straight up. I lost all power of speech and thought when, turning my head toward the grotto, I saw at one of the openings of the rock a rosebush, one only, moving as if it were very windy. Almost at the same time there came out of the interior of the grotto a golden-colored cloud, and soon after a Lady, young and beautiful, exceedingly beautiful, the like of whom I had never seen, came and placed herself at the entrance of the opening above the rosebush. She looked at me immediately, smiled at me and signed to me to advance, as if she had been my mother. All fear had left me but I seemed to know no longer where I was. I rubbed my eyes, I shut them, I opened them; but the Lady was still there continuing to smile at me and making me understand that I was not mistaken. Without thinking of what I was doing, I took my rosary in my hands and went on my knees. The Lady made a sign of approval with her head and herself took into her hands a rosary which hung on her right arm. When I attempted to begin the rosary and tried to lift my hand to my forehead, my arm remained paralyzed, and it was only after the

Lady had signed herself that I could do the same. *The Lady left me to pray all alone; she passed the beads of her rosary between her fingers but she said nothing; only at the end of each decade did she say the 'Gloria' with me.*[3]

"When the recitation of the rosary was finished, the Lady returned to the interior of the rock and the golden cloud disappeared with her.

"As soon as the Lady had disappeared Jeanne Abadie and my sister returned to the grotto and found me on my knees in the same place where they had left me. They laughed at me, called me imbecile and bigot, and asked me if I would go back with them or not. I had now no difficulty in going into the stream, and I felt the water as warm as the water for washing plates and dishes.

" 'You had no reason to make such an outcry,' I said to Jeanne and Marie while drying my feet; 'the water of the canal is not so cold as you seemed to make believe!'

" 'You are very fortunate not to find it so; we found it very cold.'

"We bound up in three fagots the branches and fragments of wood which my companions had brought; then we climbed the slope of Massabieille and took the forest road. Whilst we were going toward the town I asked Jeanne and Marie if they had noticed anything at the grotto.

" 'No,' they answered. 'Why do you ask us?'

" 'Oh, nothing,' I replied indifferently.

"However, before we got to the house, I told my sister Marie of the extraordinary things which had happened to me at the grotto, asking her to keep it secret.

---

[3] According to Mère Marie Alphonse, the Superior of the Hospital Bernadette when I was there in 1939, this observation was soon regarded as extremely significant and aroused the first suspicions regarding the identity of the Beautiful Lady. The *Pater Noster* and the *Ave* would logically be omitted by one who had no need to pray for her daily bread and who would certainly not salute herself, while, on the other hand, she would gladly glorify the Trinity.

"Throughout the whole day the image of the Lady remained in my mind. In the evening at the family prayer I was troubled and began to cry.

" 'What is the matter?' asked my mother.

"Marie hastened to answer for me and I was obliged to give the account of the wonder which had come to me that day.

" 'These are illusions,' answered my mother; 'you must drive these ideas out of your head and especially not go back again to Massabieille.'

"We went to bed but I could not sleep. The face of the Lady, so good and so gracious, returned incessantly to my memory, and it was useless to recall what my mother had said to me; *I could not believe that I had been deceived.*"

Her conviction of this was unshakable. She went on to describe the Beautiful Lady in detail.

"She has the appearance of a young girl of sixteen or seventeen. She is dressed in a white robe, girdled at the waist with a blue ribbon which flows down all around it. A yoke closes it in graceful pleats at the base of the neck; the sleeves are long and tight-fitting. She wears upon her head a veil which is also white; this veil gives just a glimpse of her hair and then falls down at the back below her waist. Her feet are bare but covered by the last folds of her robe except at the point where a yellow rose shines upon each of them. She holds on her right arm a rosary of white beads with a chain of gold shining like the two roses on her feet."

It cannot astonish anyone, in view of the experience which, however inexplicable, seemed so real to Bernadette, that she should have wished to return to the grotto. She recovered quickly from her first stunned surprise; what she felt next was eager anticipation—for she no more doubted that she would see the Beautiful Lady again than she believed that the first vision had been merely an illusion. But she met with no cooperation in her project. Her mother, at first casually, and then angrily, forbade her return to the scene of the phenomenon; Louise believed that if this had not been imaginary, then it was almost certainly demoniacal.

Bernadette then enlisted the support of her sister Toinette and her friend Jeanne Abadie. At first Louise refused to listen to them no less angrily than she had replied to Bernadette; but at last, on Sunday,[4] she gave way. She was probably sick of the subject; certainly she was disgusted rather than inspired by it.

The three little girls started out, armed with a vial of holy water; if what their elders said was true, they might need this to ward off malign influences. Before they had progressed very far on the path through the forest which they had chosen, they were joined by various playmates; for, though Bernadette had told no one outside her family what she was sure had happened, her sister had chatted freely about it, here, there and everywhere. Some of the additional children decided, rather tardily, that they should dress up for such an important occasion and asked Jeanne to wait for them. The result was that Bernadette, who had paid no attention to this importunity and who walked more rapidly than her sister and the remaining children, reached the grotto first; she knelt down before it and began to pray. The next contingent had hardly caught up with her when Bernadette called back to them.

"There she is! There she is!"

They strained forward eagerly, but they could see nothing except the same rosebush which had always been there. However, the atmosphere seemed strangely electrified, and Marie Hillot, the little girl to whom the vial of holy water had been entrusted, handed it to Bernadette and whispered excitedly, "Throw it at her!" Bernadette took the vial calmly and, instead of throwing its contents in the direction of the rosebush, poured the water quietly on the ground. Then she turned and told her companion that, judging by the Beautiful Lady's smile, the latter was pleased by this action. After that, Bernadette apparently forgot the other children completely; she was again absorbed in a beatific vision, and her

---

[4] Second apparition, February 14, 1858.

withdrawal from them and her fixed gaze toward a point which seemed to them quite unchanged was vaguely disturbing. Nevertheless, except for a minor incident, to which, ordinarily, no one would have paid any attention, this second visit might have brought the curiosity about Bernadette's alleged experiences to an end. It was natural that the community should have been roused temporarily by her story; but some trifling gossip would probably have soon overshadowed it, if a stone had not come noisily tumbling down the incline where the grotto was located and splashed into the river. Before Jeanne Abadie, who was just arriving with the last of the stragglers, could explain that she had thrown the stone herself, for fun, the others had scattered in every direction, screaming for help as they ran. Their cries quickly resounded in the nearby mill, and Nicolau, the miller, and his wife and sister rushed to the rescue. They, too, had heard the talk about Massabieille and were now convinced that something untoward had, indeed, happened there. They led Bernadette, who made no resistance, and who still seemed to be more or less in a trance, back to the mill with them and detained her there, speaking to her in a soothing way; but the other children pelted on back to town. When Toinette reached the *cachot* and poured out her incoherent tale, her mother, more enraged than ever, seized a switch and started for the mill of Nicolau. It was only through his intervention that Bernadette escaped a sound thrashing, and, by now, the whole town was talking.

Fortunately for the unhappy little girl, one local gentlewoman of considerable prominence interpreted the apparitions in a different light from most of the townspeople. This lady, whose name was Antoinette Peyret, thought that possibly the gentle spirit of her friend Elisa Latapie, who had been president of the Lourdes branch of the Children of Mary, might have reappeared in mortal form. The dress ascribed to the Beautiful Lady by Bernadette—the traditional blue and white of the organization over which Elisa had presided—made the possibility believable, at least to Mlle. Peyret. She persuaded another friend, Mme. Millet, to visit the *cachot* with her, and the two spoke soothingly to Bernadette and compellingly to her mother. They asked Louise to permit her daughter to accompany them to the grotto, and they made the request in such a way that she could not very well decline to comply. These were persons of importance, whose visit was in itself a compliment; their belief in her child's truthfulness and faith was reassuring. It would be a very different matter for Bernadette to act as their guide from having her lead a gang of ragamuffins. If agreeable to them, Louise said respectfully, Bernadette would conduct them to Massabieille the following morning.[5]

All three went first to early Mass. Then they set out for the grotto. Mme. Millet carried a blessed candle; Mlle. Peyret pen, paper, and ink. It was the former's idea that this was an occasion of such importance that it warranted the traditional taper of Candlemas; the latter's idea was to have recorded, immediately, anything which might be said.

As a matter of fact, she heard nothing and saw nothing, and neither did Mme. Millet. But both accepted, without question, Bernadette's account of what she saw and heard. Yes, she said, the Beautiful Lady had appeared again and had spoken again. She had signified that it would not be necessary to write down her remarks; she would give them clearly, but verbally. It was not distasteful to her that other visitors had accompanied Bernadette, but she wished them to remain at a slight distance. As to the little girl, she was to return fifteen times, at regular intervals. No explicit reason was given for this command, but a definite pledge accompanied it: though she did not promise that Bernadette would be happy in this world, the Beautiful Lady gave her word that happiness would be waiting in heaven.

Apparently, Mme. Millet and Mlle. Peyret were convinced that Bernadette's vision was based on reality, and that the Beautiful Lady she

---

[5] Third apparition, February 18, 1858.

saw, though not an earthly embodiment of their lost leader, was undoubtedly a supernal being of some sort. At all events, their report was so far favorable that, for some days, no impediments were placed in the way of Bernadette's further visits to the grotto and, what was more, she persuaded her mother and her aunt to accompany her.

On her fourth and fifth visits,[6] she saw the same apparition as before. And, on the fifth, the Beautiful Lady taught her a prayer, which she continued to recite daily as long as she lived, but of which she never revealed the text. She did, however, divulge that, at the time of one of the earliest apparitions, she had been told that she should always bring a blessed candle with her, as Mme. Millet had done. At first her instructions were to take these candles home with her; afterward she was instructed to leave them behind, which she did, propping them up against a great rock. The candles which now burn perpetually at the shrine are the logical results of these initial offerings.

On the occasion of the sixth apparition,[7] she received the injunction, "Pray for sinners," which, henceforth, she never failed to do. This apparition was also noteworthy in quite a different way: Dr. Dozous, a prominent physician of Lourdes, insisted upon accompanying her and rendered signal service, both to Bernadette and to the community at large, by announcing that he could find nothing abnormal about her physical condition even when her mental state was trancelike. "Her pulse was regular, her respiration easy and nothing indicated nervous excitement," he stated openly. Nevertheless, many substantial citizens of the town were greatly concerned. A meeting was called and sharp differences of opinion were expressed regarding the apparitions. Even those gentlemen who regarded them with favor admitted that, since curious crowds were increasing rapidly in number, a certain amount of danger

[6] February 19 and 20, 1858.
[7] February 21, 1858.

attended such gatherings, albeit they were marked by no disorder. There was not much open space around the grotto, and spectators had begun to climb trees, whose branches might break, and stand on stones, with slippery surfaces, which protruded from the Gave. If any kind of an accident took place, the results might be disastrous. Since Bernadette was, in the last analysis, the cause of this potential peril, only one course was safe to pursue: she must be forbidden to go to the grotto and the person to do this was the Procureur Impérial, M. Dutour. Accordingly, she was summoned into his presence.

He did not speak to her unkindly, but he did speak positively. After telling her that she was unquestionably the victim of her imagination, he forbade her to return to the grotto and asked her to give him her word that she would refrain from doing so. But she was not in the least overawed, and she could speak firmly, too. She said she was sure she was not imagining anything and that she could not give her word to refrain from going to the grotto, because she had promised the Beautiful Lady she would do so. Surprisingly, both to M. Dutour and to Bernadette, she had the last word. He dismissed her, telling her that he would think the matter over.

Later, he repeated the conversation to a group of friends, treating it lightly. Two of them did not regard it as a laughing matter. One of them was M. Estrade, the minor government official to whom we have already referred; he was to become Bernadette's friend, as well as Dutour's, and to perform an invaluable service by listening in at future conversations and scrupulously recording them, word for word. The other was M. Jacomet, the Chief of Police, who determined to see the child himself and deal with her more conclusively than M. Dutour had been able to do. He did not even know her by sight, but the court usher did. This functionary was instructed to watch for her and bring her to the Chief without delay. As she was quietly leaving Vespers that afternoon, accompanied by her aunt, she was stopped and told to come at once to M. Jacomet's office.

She went alone and unafraid, while her aunt hurried off to alert her parents to this latest happening; and, when she was ushered into the Chief's office, she found an unexpected and helpful witness: M. Estrade had asked for the privilege of being present at the interview and, then and there, began the record which has proved so invaluable. He described her face as "round and rosy," her attitude as "natural," and her dress as "clean and neat." She was told to sit down at a desk opposite the Chief and did so, as usual calmly folding her hands in her lap. M. Jacomet, armed with pen and paper, began by asking her routine questions about her name, age, occupation, etc.; then he told her to describe the scenes at Massabieille. When she had done so, in minute detail, he made a deliberate attempt to confuse her, by pretending to understand exactly the opposite of what she had said. So this Beautiful Lady appeared to be about nineteen or twenty years of age? No, monsieur, as I told you before, she appeared to be about sixteen or seventeen. And she was dressed in blue with a white girdle? No, no, in white with a blue girdle. And so on and so on. At last, he told her that he knew more about the matter than she supposed; he had been reliably informed that she was secretly following a suggestion she should pretend she had seen the Blessed Virgin and, thereby, gain all sorts of favors. She denied the accusation, speaking as collectedly and as tranquilly as she had done all along. Then the Chief said that, if she persisted in her folly, and declined to promise that she would not return to the grotto, he would have her imprisoned. To this threat she made no reply, although M. Estrade, entering into the discussion for the first time, mildly advised her to do as she was told. Just at this point, her father, who by now had been able to act on her aunt's warning, came to the door and respectfully asked for a hearing: if the Chief would only let his daughter off this one more time, he would take her home and guarantee that there would be no further disturbances.

He believed in his guarantee and so did the Chief; Bernadette was allowed to depart in her father's charge, after both had been given a stern warning. But the inner voice which was urging her on was stronger than any earthly admonition. Though she went directly to school the next morning, on her way home in the afternoon she paused to think the matter over. After all, she had made a promise and it was a dreadful thing to break one, more dreadful than running the risk of imprisonment. She took a circuitous route, but all the same she continued on her way to the grotto.

Unfortunately, the point at which she had hesitated was almost directly opposite the police barracks and the *gendarmerie* had already received its instructions. The minute she was observed, two policemen emerged from the barracks and followed her; so did the usual crowd she attracted. The policemen did not try to prevent her progress, and when she knelt down in her accustomed place, they stood at respectful attention. But as she rose, they sprang forward and asked if she still insisted she had seen a Beautiful Lady.

"No, this time I saw nothing at all," she answered.

She was allowed to go home, but she was followed by taunts and threats. The ragtag and bobtail called out mockingly that it was quite obvious the Beautiful Lady was afraid of the police and had found some safer place to go; the *gendarmes* told her they hoped she had learned her lesson. She had, but not the one they had in mind. She had learned that, however great one's faith, it is not always rewarded by radiant visions and close communion with the supernal; there is a time for all things and this had not been one of them. But there would be another. She was so confident of this that, two days later, she went back to the grotto, and this time, instead of being molested by a mob and shadowed by the police, she was not only vouchsafed her vision, but entrusted with "three wonderful secrets."[8] She never revealed what these were.

At the time of the eighth apparition[9] came the thrice-repeated warning of "Penitence!" and, on the following day,[10] she received the order, "Drink from the fountain and bathe in it." Bernadette was puzzled; there had never been a fountain at Massabieille, or any kind of a natural spring. But, getting off her knees, she began to scratch the loose gravel off the ground which encircled her. Presently, she noticed that this was moist, and then that a little pool was forming and that bubbles were rising from it. She cupped her hands together and drank; afterward, she washed her face. The next day, the pool was overflowing and water was dripping down over the rock; the following day, the trickle had become a real stream. Of course, it was immediately said—and has been said by skeptics ever since—that the spring was there all the time, but that no one had happened to notice it, in such an unfrequented place. The fact remains that Bernadette did find it and that this was no accident; she did so as a result of a direct command.

The next order, which was given on the same day that she saw the first trickle from the pool,[11] was less baffling to Bernadette; she was told to "kiss the ground in behalf of sinners." She immediately did so, and the ubiquitous crowd which accompanied her followed her example. But afterward came two more orders that were bewildering to her and, also, somewhat troubling. The first of these, on the occasion of the eleventh apparition,[12] was that she should tell the clergy to build a chapel on the site of the grotto; the second, on the occasion of the fourteenth appari-

---

[8] Seventh apparition, February 23, 1858.
[9] February 24, 1858.
[10] Ninth apparition, February 25, 1858.
[11] Tenth apparition, February 26, 1858.
[12] February 27, 1858.

tion,[13] was that people should come to this chapel in processional form.[14] She had needed no help to scratch gravel or kiss the ground; she could do little things like that quite independently. But she could not build a chapel, and, anyway, she had been told it was the clergy who should do this. Moreover, an insignificant little peasant girl could not order more important people to form processions; the clergy would have to do this, too. She must approach the parish priest, M. l'Abbé Peyramale, and, though she had not feared the Chief of Police, she was terribly afraid of the Abbé. It took a great deal of courage for her to present herself to him, and the moment she chose did not happen to be propitious; he was pacing up and down in his garden, reading his breviary. He did not welcome the intrusion on his solitude; still less did he welcome the message the timid child brought him. He dismissed her curtly, ordering her to tell the Beautiful Lady that the Curé of Lourdes was not in the habit of dealing with mysterious strangers. If she wanted a chapel and had a right to one, she must reveal Her identity. What was more, if she did not understand the message and do as she was told, it would prove either that she was an imposter or that Bernadette was having hallucinations.

In the face of such sternness it was doubly hard for Bernadette to go to the *abbatiale* three days later to talk about the matter of the processions; but, though she shrank from doing so, she persevered—only to receive much the same order as before, still more severely couched. The number of times she had promised to return regularly to the grotto was now almost complete, and the curiosity which her story aroused had spread far beyond the limits of Lourdes. When she went to Massabieille

[13] March 2, 1858.

[14] The twelfth and thirteenth apparitions, February 28, and March 1, 1858, were not marked by any extraordinary instructions or events, though, in both cases, large numbers of persons were present and, on the second, Bernadette acceded to the request made by one of these to substitute the onlooker's rosary for her own. The substitution was, apparently, not favorably received by the Beautiful Lady and the borrowed rosary was returned.

on the fourth of March,[15] her companions were no longer her childhood friends or the hoodlums of the neighborhood. The Mayor had paid an official visit to the Commandant of the Fort, and the latter had called out the entire garrison, which presented itself, in full dress uniform, at the former's office very early in the morning. The soldiers were then stationed, at intervals, along the road to Massabieille, and were reinforced by the *gendarmerie*, some of it mounted. The Mayor, the Deputy Mayor, and the Chief of Police were all very much in evidence; they wore full regalia and, far from remaining aloof, mingled with the assembled throng, which had reached the almost unbelievable proportions of twenty thousand persons ranged on either side of the road. When Bernadette appeared, a murmur arose and swelled into a singsong, "She is coming! She is coming!" A path was cleared for her, and the soldiers who accompanied her did so with respect; but, as a matter of fact, she had no need of the protection provided by their drawn swords. The multitude was hushed with awe. From the beginning, those who saw her at the grotto had been impressed with the ethereal quality of her beauty when she knelt at prayer; now this was more marked than ever, and there were greater numbers to see it. But they saw nothing else, and they heard nothing at all, except the words which Bernadette spoke as she rose from her knees and made her way back to her home through the cleared passage. Yes, she said, in answer to the questions with which she was plied, she had seen the Beautiful Lady. Yes, she meant to continue coming to the grotto; she believed the Beautiful Lady would be there again, because nothing had been said in the nature of a farewell.

Inevitably, there was a revulsion of feeling. Not that the crowds became violent; but the murmurings with which they dispersed were those of disappointment and disillusion. True, they had seen a chubby little peasant girl transfigured with strange radiance; but they had hoped

[15] Fifteenth apparition.

to share her vision, to hear the same voice that she did; they had expected that, at the very least, the rosebush would burst into sudden miraculous bloom. The tumult and the shouting had, indeed, died; the local equivalent of captains and kings had departed. But the "ancient sacrifice" of a "humble and contrite heart" still survived in Bernadette. The great revelation which was its reward was still to come. It came to her when she was alone.

On the Feast of the Annunciation,[16] M. Estrade, now recognized by Bernadette as her firm friend, was sitting quietly at home with his sister, during the late afternoon, when the child burst in upon them. She had been back to the grotto, as she had intended; and, this time, when she had implored the Beautiful Lady to reveal her identity, there had been an answer. It had come through clearly enough; but Bernadette was not sure she knew the meaning of the spoken words, which were, "*Que soy era Immaculado Conceptiou.*"[17] What did *Conceptiou* mean?

Yes, of course she had heard that term before, in connection with the Holy Mother. But it had made no particular impression upon her. The doctrine which Pius IX defined had been proclaimed an article of faith only four years earlier. It was neither understood nor discussed among persons of Bernadette's station in life She was very happy, but she was in need of enlightenment.

It came to her in many ways. The kindly Estrades did their best to explain to her, and people who needed no explanations served to make the great meaning clear by flocking to Lourdes in larger numbers than ever before. It appeared that the time had come for further official action. Baron Massy, the Prefect of Tarbes—the nearest place of any size—who was responsible for order in the entire *département* where Lourdes is located, was consulted by its Mayor. The Baron, somewhat

---

[16] Sixteenth apparition, March 25, 1858.
[17] Bigourdane dialect—"I am the Immaculate Conception."

irked by what he considered an unnecessary annoyance, gave orders that the troublesome girl should be examined by three eminent physicians, and that Dr. Dozous, who was evidently prejudiced in her favor, should not be among these. The Prefect was even more irked when the report came to him that, as far as these eminent physicians could discover, the young girl in question was both physically and mentally sound. And the Mayor continued to harass him with information and questions: crowds were increasing in number all the time, but they were orderly. Perhaps they would decrease after Easter. Meanwhile, as long as "public tranquillity and order" remained undisturbed, His Honor supposed that no suppression was necessary. If the Prefect thought otherwise, the Mayor would be glad of instructions. . . .

None was immediately forthcoming, and perhaps the crowds might have decreased after Easter if another phenomenon had not occurred on the seventh of April.[18] Bernadette had never failed to bring a lighted candle with her to the grotto since she had first been instructed by the Beautiful Lady to do so. On this occasion, holding one in her left hand as she knelt in a trancelike state, she unconsciously made a movement with her right hand which brought it into the range of the candle flame; its point appeared above her fingers and its radiance blazed through the translucency of her flesh. But Bernadette did not even hear the cries of horror which arose; she went on praying for at least a quarter of an hour, while the burning light continued to gleam through her hand. Then she emerged, as quietly as usual, from her abstraction, no more scorched than disturbed. Thereupon, Dr. Dozous, who was present, decided that he should make an experiment: he took another candle and, without any warning, thrust its lighted tip into her hand. Immediately, she cried out in pained amazement. "You are burning me!" She could not understand why her faithful friend should treat her in such an inhuman fashion.

---

[18] Seventeenth apparition.

Not unnaturally, this incident resulted in another letter from the Mayor to the Prefect: the grotto was becoming an unauthorized place of public worship, His Honor explained; it was necessary that both civil and ecclesiastical permission for such worship should be obtained. The Prefect, thus further importuned, called upon the Bishop, asking him to put an end to all this nonsense. The Bishop did not regard the matter as nonsense, nor could he be coerced into acting hastily. Until it was proven that the appearances at the grotto were unmistakably false or unmistakably true, he thought he should be guided by circumstances; he was confident that, in time, Providence would reveal the truth.

A considerable argument ensued, and, according to the meticulous M. Estrade, the parting between the Prefect and the Bishop was "stiff." Eventually, the Prefect took matters into his own hands, ordered the grotto closed and the rustic altar dismantled. Again there was murmuring, but, for the time being, the orders stood; no one tried to break through the barricade or to raise the altar again.

In a way, Bernadette was relieved that the excitement had died down; she had never desired, much less sought, to become a public figure; and now that the promised number of visits had been made and the Beautiful Lady had revealed her identity, the little girl felt no immediate compulsion to return to the grotto. Indeed, it was not until several months had passed that she wanted, or felt she needed, to go there. But on the Feast of Our Lady of Mt. Carmel,[19] as she left the altar rail after receiving Communion, she felt an irresistible urge to approach the shrine—for such she regarded it, whatever the authorities might say to the contrary. She asked her aunt to go there with her and, later in the day, received a willing assent; and, as they grew closer to the grotto, they saw that several devout women were there before them. The barricade was still in place, so they could not go as near to the spot that was sacred to them as they would have wished; but

---

[19] Eighteenth apparition, July 16, 1858.

they knelt in the grass and prayed, and, presently, all the others saw the familiar transfiguration in Bernadette and knew that she had once more recaptured her vision. It was already evening, and the quietude so beloved by the little shepherdess continued to enfold them after the radiance of the day was gone and the shadows began to fall. Though she never saw the Beautiful Lady again, the radiance that came from another source lasted all her life.

It is impossible, within the scope of a short sketch like this, to so much as suggest other phases of Bernadette's life, much less to dwell on them; it is probably superfluous to do so, in any case, as many of them are now a familiar part of history, though I have many moments of regret that the story of Bernadette's role as a shepherdess at Bartrès, and the story of her stay in Nevers, where she spent the last twelve years of her short life as a nun, are not more frequently interwoven with the story of the apparitions at Lourdes. There are, however, several aspects of these which seem to carry with them a definite message.

The first is embodied in the editorial I have already quoted: that God chooses His Own time and occasion for miracles, but that these are most frequently performed through some meek and lowly medium in a place where His Mother is honored and venerated: such a medium as Bernadette, such a place as Lourdes.

The second significant message lies in the fact that it was, to a very large degree, due to Bernadette that the doctrine of Pius IX, proclaimed only four years prior to the apparitions, became widely known among the masses. As I have said before, a century ago, persons of her station in life, though they were vaguely familiar with the term, "Immaculate Conception," rarely either understood or discussed this. After the pronouncement, made by the Blessed Virgin Herself, in the local dialect, the situation changed; the doctrine of the Immaculate Conception *did* become a matter of general discussion, and people in the community began—dimly at first, but little by little with increasing clarity—to understand that Our Lady "in the first instant of the conception was, by a singular grace and privilege of Almighty God in view of the merits of Jesus Christ, the Saviour of the human race, preserved exempt from all stain of original sin . . . Her soul at the very moment of its creation and infusion into Her body was clothed in sanctifying grace."[20] These discussions and this understanding soon spread far beyond the Département of Hautes-Pyrénées, where Lourdes is located: for instance, across the Pyrénées into Spain, where the subject had long been a matter of pious belief, beautifully interpreted by Murillo and other great painters, even though it was not a matter of dogma; throughout Italy, where Bernadette was logically regarded as a messenger divinely chosen to spread the pronouncement of a beloved Pope; throughout France, where the appearance of the Virgin before the children of Salette, only twelve years earlier, had alerted the people for further manifestations, which they eagerly anticipated and awaited; then, gradually, throughout the world. Of course, there are, to this day, persons who confuse the Immaculate Conception with the normal human birth of the Virgin and with the Virgin Birth of Christ; but their number is decreasing all the time, while the number of devotees to the Blessed Mother in this special role is increasing. The apparitions granted to Bernadette undoubtedly speeded and expanded both accurate comprehension and further devotion.

The third aspect of the apparitions to carry a definite message is, of course, the one connected with miraculous healing, both mental and physical. Lourdes has become a leading shrine—perhaps the leading shrine— for the halt, the lame, and the blind from all parts of the world. Its efficacy in certain cases cannot be doubted, even by the most skeptical. The condi-

---

[20] *A Catholic Dictionary*, edited by Donald Attwater. The Macmillan Company, New York.

tion of every sufferer going there for treatment must first be certified by his own parish priest and his own personal physician; and the official board that passes on alleged cures is composed of unimpeachable doctors of many nationalities, non-Catholic, as well as Catholic, and even non-Christian. Under these circumstances, false claims of miracles are practically impossible, and the testimonies that these have taken place are irrefutable.

There is one other aspect of the case, however, which seems to me important and which, as far as I know, has not often been stressed: this is the fact that all but the last two apparitions occurred between Sexagesima Sunday and Easter—that is to say, within a total period of a little more than seven weeks—and that, even allowing for the others, the visions lasted only from February to July—that is to say, five months. Yet, as I have just observed, their radiance sufficed to illumine Bernadette's entire life, as the knowledge of them has continued to illumine the lives of millions ever since. I believe we are very prone to feel that a privilege or a source of joy or a blessing does not amount to much unless it is prolonged; we do not, as a rule, feel thankful for every day which brings one and dwell on the memory of it with gratitude. We do not accept the arid stretches of our existence with marked resignation or philosophy, still less the painful and tragic stretches. I believe that if we ponder the story of Bernadette and take it to heart, this will help us to do so.

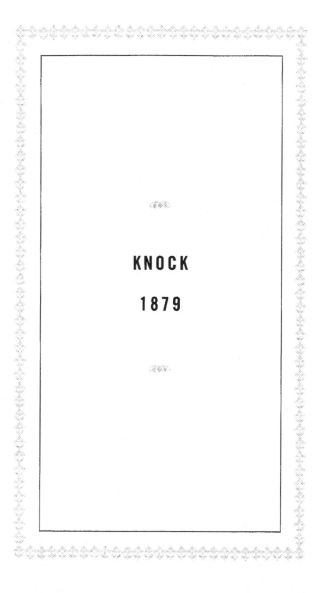

KNOCK

1879

OUR LADY
OF SILENCE

Mary Purcell

In silence and in hope shall your strength be.

ISAIAH 30:15

Knock, a remote village in the west of Ireland, stands on a wind-swept height overlooking the flat country of southeast Mayo—hence its name, a derivation of the Gaelic word *Cnoc*, a hill. Except for an occasional lake or brown patch of water-logged bogland the landscape is monotonous and uninteresting, very different from the glorious panorama of mountain, lake, and rugged coast lying farther west. From Knock on clear days the summit of Cruach Pádraig, where St. Patrick drove a hard bargain with heaven on behalf of the Irish, can be glimpsed on the western horizon. On "soft" days Atlantic rains sweep inland across Connemara where the Twelve Pins mountains shoulder one another toward the sea.

Local tradition holds that St. Patrick, halting at Knock on one of his missionary journeys, blessed the place and foretold that it would one day become a center of devotion, drawing multitudes from far and near. That prophecy has been fulfilled; no day of the year finds Knock without pilgrims; on organized pilgrimages as many as fifty thousand participate; and not only the Irish but Catholics from many lands come to pray at this shrine, one of the last Marian outposts of the Western world. They come because they believe that the Mother of God honored the little Mayo village by appearing there in 1879. During the eight decades that have since elapsed many favors and graces have been granted at Knock. Significantly, the Gaelic name for this place of Our Blessed Lady's predilection has changed over the years; it is now *Cnoc Mhuire*—Mary's Hill.

Eighty years ago Knock was an out-of-the-way hamlet, a hill on a lonely plain. Earlier in the nineteenth century when railroads began to crisscross Ireland, the Dublin-Newport mail coach ceased to run on the highway a mile south of the village; from then on Knock came to be regarded as a remote, inaccessible spot, a place "of forgotten fields and forlorn farmhouses," consisting of a dozen or more humble homes clustered about a little square-towered church. The times were bad. Small holdings of poor, undeveloped land, the exactions of rack-renting landlords, some of whom never set foot in Ireland, the cruelties of their merciless, grasping agents, evictions, emigrations, recurring famines and fevers, general misery and desolation—such was the background to rural life in the Ireland of those days. Few Irish counties were as hard hit as Mayo, and the people of Knock suffered their share of hardship, no less than eighteen destitute families in the area being evicted from their wretched cabins about the time of the apparition.

Knock church, focal point of the united parishes of Knock and Aghamore, had been built half a century before, in 1829, when Irish Catholics obtained some measure of freedom to practise their religion. Unaccustomed to anything but persecution—the pattern of which changes so little from age to age—Ireland's Underground Church when it emerged after three centuries in hiding was timid, as lacking in drive as in monetary resources. Yet the task of reorganizing religion was at once faced. In Knock as in hundreds of similar country parishes, the people, before seeking to improve their own sadly inadequate dwellings, set about building a house for God.

The poor church of Knock, with its flagged floor and accommodation to seat about thirty persons, was dedicated to St. John the Baptist. An inscription on the west wall read:

My house shall be called the house of prayer to all nations.
This is the gate of the Lord: the just shall enter into it.

A few small windows let in what light there was; the sanctuary lamp burned before an unadorned altar; there were statues of Our Lady and St. Joseph. After the coming of Archdeacon Cavanagh in 1867, a statue of St. Aloysius was added, supplied no doubt by the Archdeacon himself, whose second name was Aloysius. Father Cavanagh was a saintly man; he was deeply devoted to Our Lady's Immaculate Conception and was fond of referring to her as "the ever Immaculate Mother of God." He was known to have sold on one occasion his watch, on another his horse, to relieve the famine-stricken. "He had no banking account," says an obituary notice, "for he never had anything to put into one. All that he ever had went to the poor." But though his church lacked rich ornament, Archdeacon Cavanagh's parishioners were not wanting in either faith or hope; poor in earthly goods, they were well endowed with those treasures of grace which neither rust nor moth can consume—nor thieves steal.

In 1878, the year before the event that was to make Knock famous, a great storm partially wrecked the little church of St. John the Baptist. The slate roof and the windows were badly damaged and the statues smashed. Two new statues were at once ordered, but these got broken in transit from Dublin. It seemed as though some evil power were working to prevent the restoration of the church. But Archdeacon Cavanagh was not the man to be daunted by storms or accidents; his church could not be left without an image of Our Lady. He at once ordered two more statues, one of them a statue of Our Lady of Lourdes; these arrived safely and were duly installed after the roof had been repaired. The Archdeacon also had great devotion to the Souls in Purgatory and in May 1879 he commenced to offer one hundred Masses for them; this act of charity he completed on the very morning of the most memorable day Knock was ever to know.

Life took its usual course in the village on Thursday, August 21, 1879. Some of the inhabitants spent the forenoon making hay, others were busy bringing home turf from the bog and stacking it for winter fuel. During the afternoon clouds began to roll in from the Atlantic, and first a fine mist, then a heavy drizzle shrouded the countryside; by seven in the evening there was a steady downpour and all work in the open had to be abandoned. Archdeacon Cavanagh, who had been visiting parishioners in outlying districts, arrived home drenched through. His housekeeper, Mary McLoughlin, soon had a turf fire blazing in his living room and he sat there, drying as best he could his wet clothes. At about half past eight the housekeeper left the presbytery to visit a friend, Mrs. Margaret Beirne. Her route took her past the church. She noticed strange figures and an altar outside the church gable and wondered had the Archdeacon purchased more statues and if so, why on earth he had left them out in the rain. She also saw a white light about them but, probably attributing this to some effect of the rain and the evening light, she made no move to investigate.

Though she "thought the whole thing very strange" Mary McLoughlin dismissed the matter from her mind and went her way. Had she known it, two others had already done the same. A Mrs. Carty, passing by Knock church more than an hour before, had seen the statues; her reaction was "Another collection, God help us!"; she too proceeded on her journey without further thought. Margaret Beirne, a girl of sixteen, daughter of the woman whom Mary McLoughlin was to visit, went to lock the church—a duty usually seen to by her brother Dominick, who was sacristan—around half past seven. Having done so she was about to return home when she saw "something luminous" at the south gable. But "it never entered my mind to see what it was." She hurried home and made no mention there of the light at the church. Neither did Mary McLoughlin, when she arrived at the Beirnes', refer to what she had seen on her way there; Mary seems to have been a matter-of-fact, levelheaded person, one who would make no statement until sure of her facts.

At least three families named Beirne, a variant of the name Byrne, lived in Knock village. Mrs. Margaret Beirne, whom the Archdeacon's housekeeper came to visit, was known locally as the Widow Beirne to distinguish her from the other Mrs. Beirnes. Besides young Margaret, her son Dominick, just turned twenty, and Mary, an older daughter, lived with her. Catherine Murray, eight-year-old child of a married daughter, was also at the Beirne home that evening. The family was highly respected in the district; they were industrious and more comfortably circumstanced than many of their neighbors; three of the young people's uncles were priests in Tuam Archdiocese.

One reason why Margaret Beirne and Mary McLoughlin said nothing of what they saw at the church may have been that there was plenty to talk about in Beirnes' that evening. Mrs. Beirne herself had just returned with others from Lecanvey, a small fishing village near the foot of Cruach Pádraig where they had spent a holiday. Such a vacation would be regarded as a very tame affair nowadays, but then it was the height of adventure for country folk from inland areas to make a journey of some forty miles and remain for a few weeks by the sea. Mrs. Beirne had to hear all that had happened in Knock during her absence; the latest and worst news was that Mrs. Campbell was very ill, hardly expected to last the night; neighbors were taking turns keeping watch with Judith Campbell at her dying mother's bedside. The holiday-makers told of what life was like in faraway Lecanvey. Having heard the travelers' tales, Mary McLoughlin rose to return to the presbytery, Mary Beirne offering to accompany her part of the way.

They set off together in the rain and were just at the wall surrounding the church grounds when Mary Beirne cried, "Look at the beautiful figures! When did the Archdeacon put those statues at the gable?" Mary McLoughlin replied that whoever put them there, it certainly was not the Archdeacon. As they got nearer they noticed an extraordinarily brilliant light which surrounded the gable wall of the church and the figures standing there. "They are not statues; they are moving. It's the Blessed Virgin!" said Mary Beirne. Both girls stood motionless looking at "such a sight as you never saw in your life." Between the wall enclosing the church grounds and the church itself was an uncut meadow; three persons were seemingly standing on top of the tall grass, about a foot or two from the snow-bright gable wall. They could not be statues, as their feet did not press down the meadow grass that supported them. The south wind that rustled the rain-laden leaves and swished through the meadow did not, Mary McLoughlin noted, wet the gable or the ground beneath it. The girls at once identified the central figure as Our Lady, that on her right as St. Joseph; the third figure so greatly resembled a statue of St. John the Evangelist which Mary Beirne had seen in Lecanvey church—except that he now wore a miter, whereas the statue had shown him bareheaded—that she at once recognized him. It was still daylight. The two Marys continued to gaze in wonder at the sight until the housekeeper, more practical than her companion, told Mary Beirne to call her family.

Mary rushed home and told her mother and brother and little Catherine to hurry to the church for the Blessed Virgin was there, standing at the gable. Dominick, noticing her air of high excitement, thought that she might be the victim of fantasy or illusions and sharply told her not to be making a fool of herself. She only waited to reply, "Come and see for yourself," before dashing off to the other houses in the village to spread the good news. Dominick Beirne did not like it, he told his mother, and begged her to follow Mary and fetch her home "before she makes a show of herself before all the neighbors." Mrs. Beirne decided to go to the church, and within a short time she and Dominick and Catherine Murray were standing beside Mary McLoughlin; soon Catherine went flying back to the Beirne home to call Aunt Margaret, who had not been in the house when Mary brought word of the wonderful sight. In all, about eighteen people, most of them now only names to us, saw the apparition. Fourteen gave evidence before the Diocesan Commission which examined them two months later; these included three men, two children, two teen-age boys and a girl, and six women, their ages ranging from six to seventy-five. Another man of some sixty years who lived about half a mile from Knock also came before the Commission to tell of the large globe of golden light he had seen on the night of August 21. He had been walking in his fields about nine o'clock and saw this great light covering the whole gable of Knock church; at the time he thought that someone had been foolish enough to make a fire in the grounds of the church; next day when he inquired of neighbors if they had seen the brilliant light which was stationary over the church for so long a period the previous night, he was told of the apparition.

What exactly did they see, those favored ones whose evidence was later accepted as "trustworthy and satisfactory" by the priests deputed to examine them on behalf of the Church? They saw the south gable of Knock church suffused and covered with a brilliant golden light, a light that sparkled, making the night as bright as noonday, a changing light that sometimes mounted, lighting the sky above and beyond the gable, and sometimes subsided and got whiter and more brilliant, so that the gable seemed like a wall of snow. Within this luminous area—made all the brighter because of the rainy leaden skies and the night shadows closing in—everyone who came, including those whose business took them the road through Knock that evening, saw the apparition. They stood there silent, praying, watching, taking in the details which in the first moment of amazed delight escaped them.

To the rear of the three figures they saw an altar with a large cross in front of which a young lamb stood, "face to the west." One boy saw angels "hovering during the whole time, for an hour and a half or longer; I saw their wings fluttering, but not their heads or faces which were not turned to me." The small boy, John Curry, saw "two angels flying back and forth." An elderly man noted carvings of angels and saints on the lower portion of the altar. Some saw a cross behind the lamb, some lights, one a halo of stars.

The three figures were clothed in dazzling white raiment that shone like silver. Our Lady's robe, strikingly white, was covered by a large white cloak that fastened at the throat and fell in ample folds to her ankles. On her head was a brilliant crown surmounted with glittering crosses and over the forehead where the crown fitted the brow was a beautiful rose. She held her hands extended apart and upward, in a position that none of the witnesses could have previously seen in any statue or picture, "in the same position as a priest holds his hands when praying at holy Mass." Her gaze was fixed on the heavens; she did not look at any time toward the group gathered near the gable; nor at thirteen-year-old Patrick Hill or the child John Curry, or Judith Campbell, the three of whom went inside the wall and right up near the gable. She appeared to be praying. Three of those present noticed her bare feet; one old Gaelic-speaking woman, Bridget Trench, who had been on her knees exclaiming over and over, "A hundred thousand thanks to God and to the Glorious Virgin for showing us this sight," was so entranced that she went toward the gable to embrace the Virgin's feet. But her arms closed on empty air. "I felt nothing in the embrace but the wall, yet the figures appeared so full and so lifelike and so lifesize that I could not understand it and wondered why my hands could not feel what was so plain and distinct to my sight." Like Mary McLoughlin, Bridget remarked how heavily the rain was then falling. "I felt the ground carefully with my hands, and it was perfectly dry. The wind was blowing from the south, right against the gable, but no rain fell on that portion of the gable where the figures were." She remained there telling her beads for over an hour, full of joy; and was "so taken with the Blessed Virgin" that she did not pay much attention to the other figures.

St. Joseph stood on Our Lady's right, his head bent toward her as though bowed in respect and devotion. He had more color in his face than the other figures; his hair and beard were gray; "he looked old." He was at the extreme left (looking from the road) of the gable, and St. John, who was slightly to the right of the gable, was standing at an angle to Our Lady and at the Gospel side of the altar behind him. He was dressed as a Bishop, but wore a short miter rather than the usual high Bishop's miter. He held a large open book in his left hand while he kept the fingers of his right hand raised as though preaching or teaching. Patrick Hill went so close that he saw the lines and letters in the book. He thought the Evangelist appeared to be preaching, but he heard no voice. None of the three spoke; neither did the watchers speak; they remained silent, praying each in his or her own way. The sacristan, Dominick Beirne, was filled with wonder and so overcome that he shed tears.

All this time "it was teeming, pouring rain." The Widow Beirne left after a quarter of an hour. Mary McLoughlin remained for an hour, then hurried back to the low, thatched, and whitewashed cottage that did duty for presbytery and told the parish priest of the wonderful sight to be seen at the church; she suggested that it would be worth his while to go there. "But he appeared to make nothing of what I said and did not go." He said that it might be the reflection of one of the two stained-glass windows. The other witnesses were still at the church, though their clothes were soaked through by this time. After eleven o'clock (present Irish time) all the men and boys except Dominick Beirne went away. So did old Bridget Trench, who would not have gone only that she was sure the vision and the brightness would remain there always. "I thought that when I came back I would again behold them; when I first saw the apparition I thought I could never leave the spot and I would not have left so soon had I known that by next day all would have vanished."

Judith Campbell, probably conscience-stricken at the thought that her dying mother might be alone, was next to go. In a few minutes she rushed back crying that her mother was dead. At once those who were still watching and praying at the church hurried to the Campbells'. The sick woman had evidently made an attempt to drag herself out of bed and toward the church and had collapsed on the threshold. She was unconscious but not dead. Kind hands soon lifted her back to bed and remained to give what assistance they could; Mrs. Campbell, in fact, lived until the following day. Dominick and Mary Beirne then returned to the church; it was about a quarter past eleven; but there was nothing to be seen, only the driving rain lashing the ground and the gable that had been so dry before.

Next morning Archdeacon Cavanagh said Mass as usual; it was the octave day of the Assumption. Afterward he was told of the previous night's wonderful happening and remembered the scant notice he had paid his housekeeper's story. A possible explanation for his unreadiness to believe Mary McLoughlin may have been the fact that Mary, though a jewel among priests' housekeepers, was known to have "a little fault." Following an illness she had begun to take stimulants as a tonic; the tonic became a habit and there were a few years during which Mary McLoughlin occasionally drank a little more than was fitting for a presbytery housekeeper. When she returned with her tale of visions at the church gable, the Archdeacon may have thought that she had celebrated

Mrs. Beirne's return from Lecanvey in too convivial a manner. Now, hearing the same story from those who were at Mass, he questioned Dominick Beirne, later Mary Beirne, and others. In fairness to Mary McLoughlin it must be stated that Mary Beirne, questioned toward the end of her life concerning the housekeeper's "little fault," emphatically denied that Mary McLoughlin had had any drink that evening. She also stressed the fact that Mary's lapses from grace were only occasional and never occurred except during the few years of her partiality for "the drop."

The Archdeacon's people believed that Knock had been favored with the apparition solely because of their pastor's personal holiness and his intense devotion to Mary Immaculate. "We were *lost* [chagrined] that you were not there to see what we saw, Your Reverence," was a remark he heard on all sides that Friday morning. As he said the Office of the octave of the Assumption, not then superseded by Office for the Feast of the Immaculate Heart of Mary, he must have been on the one hand torn by distractions, on the other strangely exultant, the Antiphons, Psalms, Hymns, and Lessons taking on a fresher and more vivid meaning for the man who recited them as he walked up and down the road between his cottage and the gable wall of the church.

The news spread like wildfire, mostly by word of mouth, the local and national papers having been requested by the clergy to refrain from giving the Knock happenings much publicity. In fact, not till well over four months later did the first press report appear, by which time the story was known throughout Ireland and indeed throughout the Catholic world. Ten days after the apparition a deaf child was cured; a man born blind saw after making a pilgrimage to Knock; a dying man, so ill that he vomited blood most of the way while being carried to Knock and received the Last Sacraments from the Archdeacon on his arrival, was cured instantaneously after drinking some water in which a scrap of cement from the gable wall had been dissolved. Soon seven or eight cures were being reported each week, among them cases of paralysis, blindness, epilepsy, cancer, heart trouble, bone disease, and tuberculosis. Many attributed their cures to the use of the cement from the gable; as might be expected, the ever-increasing crowds began to take this cement away with them for sick friends at home or overseas. Thus a nun in a convent in Arabia writes thanking those who sent the scrap of cement and reports the cure of a young Sister from a wasting disease. The mother of a large family in Autun, France, is similarly cured of cancer; a Michigan lady of dropsy; a Newfoundland carpenter of a serious hand injury.

The wall of the gable was so damaged by the constant scraping and loosening of the cement that it was in danger of collapsing, and the Archdeacon had to have the lower part of the gable encased in wooden sheathing. Despite the little encouragement given to Knock by the majority of the Irish clergy, invalids were being brought there from every county in the land. A Limerick lady, daughter of well-to-do landowners, in her reminiscences of the period tells of how poor pilgrims from the south of Ireland, walking every step of the two hundred miles and more to Knock, used to get a night's shelter at her family home. One elderly man, the most pitiable of all these travelers, had a large unsightly growth on his neck which reached down to his chest. He was so weak that he could walk only with the aid of a stick and leaning on the shoulder of a young lad, a relative, who helped him along. When he left the County Limerick farmhouse for Knock, the children stood about staring in horror at the man's deformity, while their elders shook their heads, very doubtful that one so afflicted would ever get as far as Knock. Not many weeks later the same pilgrim came again on his homeward journey. He was almost unrecognizable, the growth having completely vanished; he looked well and strong. When questioned he said that he had been cured suddenly when making a "Station" at Knock.

Knock pilgrims in the early days were more or less free to perform whatever devotions they chose, the clergy holding aloof, much as the Lourdes clergy did in the early days of the Lourdes pilgrimages. The people, thus left to their own spiritual devices, reverted spontaneously to the traditional forms of Gaelic piety and devotion. They did "rounds" of the church grounds, reciting the Rosary and Litanies aloud, as their forebears of the glorious thousand years between the Patrician era and the Reformation had recited the "three fifties of the Psalms" while walking round and round some holy place. This praying while doing a slow circuit was known as doing or making "a Station." The Knock pilgrims of the eighties also kept all-night vigil on the eves of feasts of Our Lady, some went barefoot to Knock and did "Stations" on their bare knees, practices in the true ascetic tradition of the early Irish Church.

Though his fellow priests doubted and disapproved, Archdeacon Cavanagh firmly believed in the apparition right from the beginning. To the end of his life—which came on the feast of the Immaculate Conception, 1897, an appropriate day for a devoted servant of Our Blessed Lady to breathe his last—he regretted not having gone to the church when his housekeeper had suggested it on the night of the apparition. But he consoled himself with the thought that it was the will of God that the vision had been vouchsafed to the people, not the pastor. Besides, he soon realized that had he himself seen what his parishioners saw, unfavorable interpretations might have ensued. "If I had seen the apparition and if I had been the first to speak of it, many things would have been said that cannot now be advanced." Most of the clergy of Tuam Archdiocese and of Ireland in general were skeptical of the Knock apparition and thought the Archdeacon exceedingly credulous. It is true that he was of an unquestioning mind; his simple, childlike faith in the apparition and his ready acceptance of stories of cures gave some ground for the criticisms of the clergy. On the other hand it must be remembered that the Archdeacon knew his people as no one else did; the only priest in the district, he would have been confessor to most of his flock; the Gaelic word, *anam-chara,* "soul-friend," implies the regard in which the people held that spiritual relationship; he if anyone was in a position to judge whether the witnesses were truthful or not.

Within two months of the apparition the Archbishop of Tuam set up a Commission to make an official enquiry into the Knock happenings. Nine priests conducted the investigation, interrogating the witnesses separately and recording their evidence. As some critics had put forward the theory that the apparition was due to a magic-lantern projection, a science professor came from Maynooth and made tests with a magic lantern, twenty priests being present at these experiments. The Reverend professor told the Commission that his tests ruled out the possibility that someone had projected a photographic image on the gable wall. The Commission seems to have done its work thoroughly and carefully, eliciting the depositions from each witness by questioning. At the conclusion of the sittings a report was sent to the Archbishop stating that the testimony of the witnesses was trustworthy and satisfactory. The late Father Herbert Thurston, S.J., a world-famous authority on the subject of supernatural occurrences and visions, writing of Knock and the evidence given before this Commission, stated:

> I find it hard to believe that these people, simple folk of all ages, were deliberately lying when they stated that they stood or knelt for an hour or more looking at these motionless figures and the illuminated wall of the church in the pouring rain.

The then Archbishop of Tuam, Dr. McHale, was ninety years of age and in failing health; he made no statement on Knock, for or against, so the pilgrims kept on coming there.

The Commission having completed its work before the end of 1879, the newspapers considered themselves free to report and comment. First a local paper, *The Tuam News,* sent a representative to Knock and published regular accounts of the crowds and the cures. Early in 1880 the Dublin *Weekly News* reporter went there and reported the traffic congestion in the little village: vehicles of all kinds were drawn up at both sides of the road while masses of people milled to and fro. He saw men and boys mounting on the shoulders of others to prize loose fragments of cement from the upper portion of the gable wall, while hats and hands were stretched from beneath to catch the tiniest scrap that might fall. What had been an uncut meadow five months previously was now a slough of mire three inches deep. People were kneeling, standing, walking, completely absorbed in prayer, some in the precincts of the church, some on the roadway and the fields beyond. Booths had been set up, presumably for the sale of food and religious objects. Around the gable there was always a great crowd, some of whom prayed silently, some aloud.

The London *Daily Telegraph* also sent a correspondent who was vastly interested in the magic-lantern theory, a theory already demolished by the Maynooth professor. He made his own practical tests and reported to his paper that "however the reported apparitions were caused, they could not have been due to a magic lantern." This gentleman sought interviews with some of the witnesses and was very impressed with young Patrick Hill, whom he found "bright and intelligent; a little fellow who told his tale clearly and simply." Indeed all the newspapermen thought highly of Patrick, whose home was in the town of Claremorris, six miles away, but who happened to be visiting with an aunt in Knock at the time of the apparition; young Hill answered all the reporters' questions frankly and readily; he was the boy, it will be remembered, who went right up to the gable and observed everything close at hand; he looked into St. John's book; he noticed the beautiful rose on Our Lady's brow; he saw the angels' wings. He died in Boston about 1927 without ever having retracted one detail of his evidence; it seems a pity that he did not live longer or that the 1936 examination of the surviving members of the group examined in 1879 was not held a decade earlier. Mary Beirne was another witness interviewed by the pressmen; she was a courteous and very intelligent person, giving straightforward answers to all questions, drawing no attention to her own important part as the one who first called the others and the last to leave the gable wall, anxious only that the exact truth be known.

In 1880, the year following the apparition, there were reports of further visions and strange happenings at Knock; no witness of the first apparition was involved in these later occurrences, none of which was deemed worthy of investigation. Nevertheless they received much publicity, and some newspapers reported them as deserving of acceptance. As little or no press publicity had attended the original apparition, much confusion was now created in the public mind by the fact that the counterfeit was being given equal and even greater importance than the real. Those disinclined to believe in the apparition of August 21, 1879, were now criticizing Knock; clergy who had been content to disapprove now became openly hostile. Derisive articles and letters appeared in certain Irish and English newspapers noted for their antipathy to Catholicism. Still Knock continued to draw not only individual pilgrims but organized groups, a pilgrimage of nine hundred coming from Manchester in 1882. That same year Archbishop Lynch of Toronto made the long journey to Mayo, and in 1883, Archbishop Murphy of Hobart, Tasmania, came; both these prelates were making thanksgiving for cures they had obtained through the intercession of Our Lady of Knock.

In 1881, 1882, and 1883, Mary Frances Cusack, an Anglican Sister who had entered the Church at the time of the Oxford movement and who had some reputation as a writer, visited Knock. Miss Cusack had had a rather tempestuous time in the barque of Peter; in the year following her conversion she became a Poor Clare, receiving the habit after a month's postulancy; the next year she came to a new foundation in County Kerry and for many years devoted herself to writing lives of the saints and later controversial articles, mostly on political and social questions. Unfortunately Miss Cusack, or The Nun of Kenmare, as she was commonly called from her favorite nom de plume, had an unhappy knack of rubbing people the wrong way. Her first visit to Knock took place between "flittings" from one convent to another; she tried to found a convent there and for a time was supported by Archdeacon Cavanagh, but later they disagreed and she set off first for England, then for America, to be a trial to many Bishops both sides of the Atlantic. Eventually she left the Church and wrote her autobiography, *The Nun of Kenmare*. It is interesting to note that Miss Cusack, who might be expected to discount the Knock story, and whose autobiography shows how bitter she felt about many things Catholic, expresses her firm belief in the apparition and claims to have been cured of a knee ailment there.

In 1881 this lady, with some Dublin friends, had breakfast in Mrs. Beirne's home. Her description clearly proves the Beirnes to have been what we in Ireland call "the good old stock"; she admires their good manners and their unobtrusive attention to the visitors. They were entertained "in a clean, comfortable apartment, where tea, fresh eggs, milk, butter, and fine white bread were served in abundance." After the meal a priest member of the party questioned Mary Beirne on the apparition. Miss Cusack describes Mary as "an intelligent and highly respectable girl, quiet and modest in demeanour, and evidently one of the last persons who could be influenced by imagination, or who would invent a story . . . After conversation with nearly all those who saw the apparition, I found the simplest account was that given by Mary Beirne. I do not think it would be possible even for the most hardened skeptic to doubt that she has seen the vision of which she speaks so simply, and with such gentle love of the Immaculate Mother of God."

Mary Beirne later became Mrs. O'Connell; in 1936, when in her eighty-second year, she made a statement before a board of priests reaffirming her evidence of 1879. Later in 1936 she made a sworn statement again describing what she saw the night of the apparition, ending with the words, "I am quite clear about everything I have said, and I make this statement knowing I am going before my God." Later still in the same year, when her death was imminent, yet another Commission visited her; the judges were extremely impressed with the care she took considering the questions put to her, diligently assorting her memories so that the facts she was absolutely certain of and those she was not quite sure about might not be confused. That a son of this grand old lady should have had a distinguished career in a later Ireland, leaving his impress on both educational and political fields, and that a grandson should be today in the top rank of *his* chosen profession is an interesting and—for clients of Our Lady of Knock—a gratifying aftermath.

Mary's sister, young Margaret Beirne, died the summer following the apparition. Patrick Beirne and John Curry were the other two survivors examined by the 1936 Commission. The Commission found Beirne "of a slightly difficult disposition and as it seemed to us, he considers himself a person of some importance, but nevertheless he is judged by us to be upright and truthful." Patrick Beirne was the last of the witnesses to die. John Curry was so young at the time of the apparition that when interviewed at a Home of the Little Sisters of the Poor in New York in 1936 by the New York Tribunal, he was slightly confused on some points. The convent Chaplain and the Superioress said that he was truthful and of good character, a constant Mass-server and a daily Communicant. He told the Tribunal that he remembered the two angels he saw flying back and forth and ended by saying, "I will remember what I saw that night till I die." Patrick Walsh, the man who saw the light over the gable while walking on his farm at some distance from the church, had in later life the happiness of seeing three of his sons ordained priests, a privilege accorded few fathers.

The continued opposition, particularly from the clergy, began to tell eventually, and by 1900 there was a great falling off in the number of pilgrims at Knock. Yet there was no year when pilgrims failed to come, and they came by the thousand for the Assumption vigil and feast, when extra priests had to be drafted in to minister to the numbers wishing to confess and receive Holy Communion. In 1929 the Archbishop of Tuam, for the first time, took part in the pilgrimage devotions; he referred to the Commission of 1879 and explained that since no decision had been given by the Church, Catholics were free to follow their own convictions and inclinations in regard to the apparition. This was the same Archbishop who in 1936 set up the Commission to examine the three surviving witnesses.

Since Most Reverend Dr. Walsh became Archbishop of Tuam in 1940 he has taken the cause of Knock to heart; he may be seen there on most pilgrimage days, when he himself officiates at the Blessing of the Sick. He has obtained from Rome many indulgences for the pilgrims and secured the affiliation of Knock to the Basilica of St. Mary Major in Rome. The present order of devotions at the shrine allows pilgrims to travel long distances and yet receive Holy Communion at the special afternoon Mass celebrated at 4 P.M. Outdoor Stations of the Cross, Rosary and Litany of Our Lady recited while walking in procession around the church grounds, and a short sermon precede the Mass; afterward invalid pilgrims are blessed with the Blessed Sacrament as at Lourdes; Benediction brings the devotional exercises to a close. The Knock Shrine Society, a body of voluntary helpers, was founded in 1935 to promote the cause of the Shrine. The Stewards see to the conduct of pilgrimages, direct pilgrims, and act as stretcher bearers; the Handmaids attend to the needs of the sick. The Knock Shrine Medical Bureau investigates cures, for favors of healing still take place there.

The unique features of the Knock apparition were the number of witnesses of varying ages, the absence of ecstasy, and the fact that no word was spoken, no message given. In Lourdes there was one who saw the vision, in Fatima three, at La Salette two, at Beauraing five—all children. It could of course be argued that the witnesses of the Knock apparition were, like the Indian Juan Diego, who saw Our Lady of Guadalupe on Tepeyac hill, full of faith and candor, children in the sight of heaven. Though the Knock witnesses experienced various emotions—happiness, wonder, devotion, exaltation of spirit, one being moved to tears—not one of them was rapt in ecstasy. None of them heard a word; neither did they receive any interior message or sign. That the Mother of God, who bade Bernadette pray for sinners, who had pleaded for conversion of life at La Salette, for prayer and penance at Fatima, should have remained silent to her devoted Irish children was, and still is, a stumbling block to many. There was no message, they say, so the apparition is devoid of meaning.

The very silence of the apparition is an invitation to ponder the symbolism of the altar with the Lamb and the Cross, the position and demeanor of the three figures. The altar was at the center and at a higher level than the figures, the Lamb above the altar but resting on it. Our Lady was between and somewhat above St. Joseph and St. John. She appeared as a Queen; several of the witnesses described the crown she wore; St. Joseph bowed to her, and St. John's right hand was raised in her direction; the rose on her brow recalls her title, *Mystical Rose*, the greatest contemplative who "pondered in her heart," the first of all who love God and are beloved by Him. Her gaze was uplifted as were her hands. In this connection it is interesting to note that none of the witnesses had ever seen a picture or statue showing Our Lady in this attitude, but authorities on Marian art have commented on the similarity between the description of Our Lady by the Knock witnesses and early Christian paintings in the Roman catacombs depicting the Blessed Virgin as Advocate, or *Orante*, her hands raised in prayer rather in the manner of a priest during the Canon of the Mass. Four witnesses said that she appeared to be praying. When a Queen prays it is to intercede for her people, to be their advocate, to obtain favors for them. Hence theologians have seen Mary as she appeared at Knock as the Mediatrix of All Graces. She was silent, wishing the witnesses to look beyond her to the altar and the Lamb ready for sacrifice; she looked up, inviting those present to accompany her in spirit to the Throne of God.

In a booklet, *The Secret of Knock*, Reverend Dr. M. O'Carroll, C.S.Sp., writes:

> The first lesson of the Apparition is the Mass. Everything seems to point to that—the altar with the sacrificial Lamb, the gesture of Our Lady, the presence of St. John in vestments, and the respectful attitude of St. Joseph. . . . But we may also see in the vision a reminder of another great truth connected with the Mass—the necessity of Mary's mediation and intercession and the unique character which the latter acquires because of Mary's glorious Assumption and Coronation. . . . No word was spoken, no oral message delivered. The Apparition does not bear in popular devotion a name or phrase giving a clue to its doctrinal meaning. Rather does it invite scrutiny, meditation, and a kind of holy wonder. If it is a help to Faith, as are all miraculous happenings, it also provides an exercise and a salutary discipline in that great virtue. It brings us near to God.

It is helpful, when thinking of Knock, to remember that messages can be conveyed without the aid of either the spoken or written word. A mother's gesture, her glance, her demeanor, her very silence, says much to her attentive children. At Knock the Blessed Mother, reverent, silent, adoring, showed how to pray. Would she not have prayed—she who stood there on the tall grass, robed and crowned as a Queen— would she not have prayed for the spread of that eternal and all-enfolding kingdom of Christ, "a kingdom of truth and life, a kingdom of holiness and grace, a kingdom of justice, love, and peace"? We may be permitted to think so. In our times, when silence has become almost a lost art, there is a strange attraction, a hidden message, a blessed consolation in that silence of Our Lady of Knock. The attraction is for all. The message, unspoken but unmistakable, is for those who ponder the apparition. But the consolation, the delight of the vision, was granted only to a few, to the quiet, unworldly people who came running through the rain one August evening at *Cnoc Mhuire*—Our Lady's Holy Hill.

FATIMA

1917

THE LADY

OF THE ROSARY

Msgr. William C. McGrath

Down the centuries the Blessed Mother of
God has repeatedly played a decisive role in
the saving of Christian civilization. Time
and again, when all seemed lost and the situation was literally "out of human hands," her
intervention—either through actual appearance on earth or through unprecedented
rosary crusades—has turned the tide of victory. Her efforts sometimes ended in failure.
Not that *she* could ever fail but because of the
refusal of her earthly children to play the
part assigned to them as a necessary condition of success. Among her most spectacular
victories were the defeat of the deadly Albi-
gensian heresy in the thirteenth century and,
three hundred years later, the annihilation of
the "invincible" Turkish armada at Lepanto.
Unsuccessful were her efforts to avert disas-

ter for France through her apparitions at La Salette and to prevent the spread of Communism and a Second World War through the "Peace Plan from Heaven" she gave us at Fatima.

The world situation in May 1917 weighed heavily on the heart of the Holy Father. Now well into its third year was the most deadly and destructive war the world had ever known. Europe was one gigantic battlefield. The sinking of the Lusitania on May 7, 1915, with the loss of more than twelve hundred lives, was the incident that galvanized American public opinion into support of a later declaration of war on April 6, 1917, but America's weight had not yet been felt in the conflict. At the rate of 31,000 tons a day Allied shipping was being sent to the bottom of the ocean in a sinister effort to cut the Atlantic life line. It would be a fight to the desperate finish, and nowhere on the horizon loomed any sign of hope for a war-weary and despairing world.

There are those who maintain that the Holy Father, Pope Benedict XV, died of a broken heart because of the abysmal failure of all his overtures to the Great Powers and his plans for a just and a lasting peace. Over and over again he had implored them to listen; to bring to an end "this cruel war, the suicide of Europe." On every occasion he had been rebuffed. Finally, despairing of any help from leaders determined only upon destruction and revenge, he directed his children throughout the world to join him in a fervent appeal to the Blessed Mother of God. In a stirring Pastoral letter, addressed to the Catholic world on May 5, 1917, Pope Benedict expressed his poignant grief and fatherly concern over this senseless slaughter. "We wish the petitions of her most afflicted children to be directed with lively confidence, more than ever in this awful hour, to the great Mother of God. To Mary, then, who is the Mother of Mercy and omnipotent by grace, let loving and devout appeal go up from every corner of the earth—from noble temples and tiniest chapels, from royal palaces and mansions of the rich as from the poorest hut—from every place wherein a faithful soul finds shelter—from blood-drenched plains and seas. Let it bear to her the anguished cries of mothers and wives, the wailing of innocent little ones, the sighs of every generous heart: that her most tender and benign solicitude may be moved and the peace we ask for be obtained for our agitated world."

In the spring of 1916, in the company of her cousins Francisco, aged eight, and his little sister Jacinta, aged six, Lucia Abóbora had taken their joint flocks of sheep to a section of her father's property known as the Chousa Velha, at the foot of a rocky promontory called the Cabeço.

In all the big wide world of human strength and human wisdom it would have been difficult to find individuals of lesser importance than those chosen by Heaven to play their role in the greatest spiritual drama of our generation. They were child shepherds, obscure, illiterate, "alike to fortune and to fame unknown," yet because of events that had their beginning on this spring day in 1916, their names were one day to be blazoned before the world and their memories to be enshrined in the hearts of countless millions when the strong and the wise of that world-war era had passed into oblivion.

Lucy Abóbora, aged nine, was the youngest of seven children. Her cousins Francisco and Jacinta were the last of eleven of the Marto family. Like the other poor families of their little village of Aljustrel, their folks had time for little more than the never-ending struggle to wrest a meager living from the barren and reluctant soil of one of the most stubbornly unproductive areas of the whole of Portugal. For schooling there was little time, with the result that none of the children had yet learned to read or write. There were daily chores for every member of every family, and in order to release her elder brothers and sisters for more profitable tasks around the farm and in the home, Lucy had recently been assigned the role of leadership of the little shepherd trio in caring daily for their joint flocks of sheep. Each day, in the graying dawn, they would lead them forth to the meager pastures among the bush and scrub of the rocky, barren area, and each evening they returned to their humble, unpretentious homes, next morning to repeat the process all over again.

There was nothing "different" about this fine spring morning. Another routine day in their routine lives. They had guided the flock to a field belonging to Lucy's father. While the sheep nibbled at the sparse available grass the children joined their youthful village companions in playing their childhood games of tag, jacks, and hide and seek. But before long there was a sudden change in the weather. A steady drizzle began to fall, borne in on the chilling breeze from the invisible ocean to the northwest. Hastily gathering the sheep together, they led them to the partial protection of a small wooded area while they themselves sought shelter in their well-known cave on the side of the promontory known as the Chousa Velha. It proved to be only a passing shower, but so absorbed had they become in their games that they remained inside the cave even after the sun had shone forth once again.

"We had played only a short time," wrote Lucy many years later, "when a strong wind shook the trees and above them a light appeared, whiter than the driven snow. As it approached, it took the form of a young man, transparent and resplendent with light. He began to speak. 'Fear not. I am the Angel of Peace. Pray with me.' He knelt on the ground, bowed low, and three times recited a prayer: 'My God, I believe, I adore, I hope and I love You. I ask pardon of You for those who do not believe, do not adore, do not hope and do not love You.' Then he arose and said: 'Pray this way. The Hearts of Jesus and Mary are attentive to the voice of your supplications.' "

The Angel disappeared as suddenly as he had come, leaving the children so overcome with sudden awareness of the world beyond that for a long period they were utterly oblivious to their surroundings. They remained rigidly in the same position in which he had left them. Over and over, with an intensity that permeated their whole being, they

repeated the beautiful prayer: "My God, I believe, I adore, I hope . . ."
"We felt the presence of God so intensely" wrote Lucy, "so intimately, that we dared not speak even to one another. The next day we felt ourselves still enveloped by its atmosphere. Only very gradually did its intensity diminish within us. None of us thought of speaking of this apparition or of recommending that it be kept a secret. It imposed secrecy of itself. It was so intimate that it was not easy to utter even a single word about it."

From then on, as if bound by an invisible common bond, the three children spent nearly all their time in one another's company. Each day, in the graying dawn, they attended Mass and after a frugal breakfast set out with their sheep to the best grazing land available in the meager countryside. Before noon they would return, only to set out again in the early evening after the great heat of the day had subsided. There were games galore in the shade of the fig trees, and there was the cool well, shaded by olive and almond, where they could take their rest. It was during one of those periods this otherwise uneventful day that they were suddenly startled by the sound of a voice: "What are you doing?" It was the Angel, who was again beside them. "Pray, pray a great deal," he continued. "The Hearts of Jesus and Mary have designs of mercy for you. Offer unceasingly to the Most High prayer and sacrifices."

"But how are we to make sacrifices?" It was Lucy who proffered the question.

"Offer up everything within your power as a sacrifice to the Lord in reparation for the sins by which he is so much offended and of supplication for the conversion of sinners. Thus bring down peace upon your country. I am the Guardian Angel of Portugal. More than all else, accept and bear with resignation the sufferings that God may send you."

Three times in all the Angel visited the children, the third time holding aloft a chalice with a host suspended above it. From the host drops of blood fell into the chalice cup, and, leaving both suspended in mid-air, he prostrated himself upon the ground and three times repeated this sublime prayer of reparation:

"Most Holy Trinity, Father, Son and Holy Ghost, I adore You profoundly and I offer You the most precious Body, Blood, Soul and Divinity of Jesus Christ, present in all the tabernacles of the world, in reparation for the outrages, sacrileges and indifference by which He Himself is offended. And by the infinite merits of His Most Sacred Heart and the Immaculate Heart of Mary, I beg of You the conversion of poor sinners."

The Angel then arose, gave the host to Lucy and the contents of the chalice to Francisco and Jacinta, saying:

"Take and drink the Body and Blood of Jesus Christ, horribly outraged by ungrateful men. Make reparation for their crimes and console your God."

Once more prostrating himself upon the ground, he recited three times with the children the prayer "Most Holy Trinity . . ." Then he disappeared from view.

It was Lucy who many years later described the overpowering sense of the presence of God that flooded their souls during and after this second visit of the Angel. It left them physically weak and, as it were, withdrawn entirely from their earthly surroundings. Her description reminds one of the words of the great St. Paul when he was transported to the third Heaven and tells us that he did not know whether he was in or detached from his own body. For days and even weeks they experienced a feeling of happy debility, overcome by the thought that from the hands of an Angel they had received the Body and Blood of Christ. It was Francisco, many days later, who first made reference to their overpowering experience:

"The Angel gave you Holy Communion," he said to Lucy, "but what was it that he gave Jacinta and me?"

"It was also Holy Communion," declared Jacinta, before Lucy could reply. "Didn't you see that it was the Blood that fell from the host?"

"I felt that God was in me," Francisco replied, "but I didn't know how it was." Then, prostrating himself upon the ground, he remained a long time, repeating over and over the Angel's prayer to the Blessed Trinity.

On May 13, 1917, in almost the same spot where, the year before, the Angel had appeared to them, the children were once more tending their sheep in the Chousa Velha in the section known as the Cova da Iria. They had said their Rosary, finished their meager luncheon, and begun to play when suddenly, out of an azure sky, a brilliant flash of light appeared. Fearing a storm, they were running excitedly to gather the sheep and head for shelter when another flash, this time more brilliant and arresting, literally rooted them to the spot. A vision had suddenly materialized above the branches of a small holm oak tree, and there, to their overpowering amazement, they beheld "the most beautiful Lady they had ever seen." "It was," writes Lucy, "a Lady dressed all in white, more brilliant than the sun, shedding rays of light clearer and stronger than a crystal glass filled with the most sparkling water and pierced by the burning rays of the sun."

The children's first impulse was to turn and run away, but the Lady beckoned to them and bade them come nearer. "Do not be afraid, I will not hurt you," she told them as they gazed upon her in silent ecstasy.

The beautiful Lady was clothed in a garment of purest white, which fell gracefully in soft folds to her feet and was adorned with a star near the hem of her long flowing robe. Her face was youthful, that of a girl of sixteen, of indescribable beauty and flooded with heavenly light, yet tinged with an expression of wistful sadness. Her hands, delicate and slender, were folded before her breast and held a white rosary with beads, cross, and chain of shining pearl. Her whole person was so resplendent with light that it dazzled the children's eyes, and for a long time they just stood and gazed, rooted to the spot and yet unable to utter a single word. It was Lucy who at last found courage to break the silence.

"Where do you come from?" she asked the gracious Lady, who now smiled upon them with an expression that won their hearts.

"I come from Heaven," she replied.

"And why have you come down here?" asked Lucy, with the simple directness of childhood.

"Because I want you children to come here on the thirteenth of each month at the same hour. In the month of October I shall tell you who I am and what I want you to do."

Lucy's courage and confidence were by now completely restored, and she felt utterly at home in the presence of the Lady, whose face was so loving and kind.

"Do you really come from Heaven?" she asked, and added: "Shall I go to Heaven too?"

"Yes, you will go there."

"And Jacinta?" she now asked, growing more confident with each passing moment.

"Jacinta will go to Heaven, too," the Lady replied.

"And Francisco?"

The Lady looked earnestly at the child with an expression of motherly reproach. "Yes," she replied, "Francisco, too, will go to Heaven, but he will first have to say many rosaries."

Lucy craved further reassurance regarding her childhood friends. There were the two little boys, their playmates, who had died last year.

"One is already in Heaven," the Lady told her, "and the other is in Purgatory."

"And Amelia?"

"Amelia will be in Purgatory till the end of the world."[1]

---

[1] For many years this "supposed" statement of our Lady was seriously called into question. Early books of Fatima had stated that Amelia was only seven years old for a child of that tender age the verdict would have seemed harsh, indeed. In an interview with Lucy a few years ago Father Thomas McGlynn, O.P., propounded this difficulty. Her reply seemed to clarify the question: "Amelia was eighteen years old, Father, and, after all, for one mortal sin a soul may be in Hell forever."

It was the Lady who now asked a question. It was addressed to all three of the children. "Do you wish to offer yourselves to God in order to accept all the sufferings He wishes to send you, in reparation for sin and for the conversion of sinners?"

With childlike and heroic simplicity they answered in unison: "Yes, we want to."

"Then you will suffer much," the Lady told them, "but God's grace will strengthen you." And she added: "My children, go on always saying the Rosary as you have just done."

It was the last word she spoke. Gradually, without walking but as if she were simply gliding over the ground, the beautiful Lady moved toward the East and the vision slowly melted into the sunlight.

Still awed and thrilled by the spectacle they just had witnessed, the children excitedly held a little consultation. It *was* real. It must have been real. They had all seen the beautiful Lady, and they had all heard her speak. And an identical feeling of indescribable joy had flooded their hearts as they stood before her. But they had better not tell anybody. No, it would be foolish, because nobody would believe them anyway and people would laugh and would say that they were making up the whole fantastic story.

But alas for good resolutions. Back that evening in the cozy precincts of her humble home, Jacinta broke down and told her mother the startling events of the never-to-be-forgotten day. By the following day it was the talk of the entire village, and the fears of the children were quickly verified. If deep joy had filled their hearts at the sight of the Heavenly Visitor, they were soon to taste of the suffering they had joyfully agreed to accept for the conversion of sinners. They were ridiculed and rebuked, and Lucy was given a severe beating, treated as a liar and a hypocrite even by members of her own family. Over and over they were cross-examined, ridiculed, held up to scorn, and threatened with even more drastic punishment if they persisted in denying that they had simply invented the whole impossible story. But in spite of threats and beatings and ridicule, they would not retract one iota of what little Jacinta had told her mother. It *was* true. The beautiful Lady *had really been there.* And what was more, she would be there again, every month, on the thirteenth, from now till October. She had spoken to Lucy and told her that one day they would all go to Heaven. What difference if they were punished? Hadn't they all agreed to accept whatever suffering God would send them? Perhaps this was part of it, and they could bear it in reparation for sin and for the souls of poor sinners. They could not help what people thought—or said—or did. They did know that the Lady had told them to go back on the thirteenth of June, and they were happy at the thought that they would see her once again.

There was one who refused to be swayed by the storm of ridicule and unbelief. It was Ti Marto, father of Francisco and Jacinta. From beginning to end he was a tower of strength to all three children and, in spite of his lack of formal education, proved to be a man of sound judgment, always ready to analyze the situation objectively "with malice toward none." Lucy's mother had already told the whole story to Father Manuel Ferreira, the local pastor, and Mr. Marto thought to himself that the case for the children would not be helped by her rendition of what they claimed to have witnessed. He deemed it best to go to the pastor himself, and his suspicions were soon verified. His Reverence had not been particularly impressed. In the light of subsequent events one might say, indeed, that Father Ferreira did not measure up too well to the situation. He was not merely incredulous. He was downright hostile and resentful. It was plain to see that he deplored the whole "unfortunate affair."

"If you ask me, it's just a mess," he told the distressed Ti Marto. "It's the first time in my life that I have ever had to listen to anything like this." Although taken aback by what he regarded as a rather superficial appraisal of the whole affair, good, honest Ti Marto gave voice to the first recorded words in favor of the helpless children.

"But, Father, you seem more ready to believe the lies that are being

uttered than the facts of the case. I have come to you with nothing but
the best of intentions, not to cause you any trouble but only to find out
what is best for us to do."

In nowise mollified by this honest statement of the case, the priest
was prepared rather petulantly to dismiss the whole sorry business. To
Marto's suggestion that the children be brought to him to give him their
own version of what they had seen, he answered:

"If you want to bring the children to me, do it. If not, just don't. I
leave it up to you."

Ti Marto descended the steps of the rectory veranda, obviously
pained by this utter lack of sympathy and understanding on the part of
one for whom he had such a high regard.

Meanwhile, at her own home, Jacinta was experiencing the same
attitude of hostile unbelief. As a matter of fact, a conspiracy was being
concocted by both mothers to deter their children from going through
with the whole silly affair. The great feast of St. Anthony was drawing
near, and it was always celebrated with bands and processions and the
traditional ceremony of giving away the loaves of bread. The children
were to be urged to attend this feast and to forget about the Cova da Iria.

But Jacinta was not so easily downed. Her generous and impetuous
nature prompted her to attempt to persuade her mother to accompany
them and to be there when the Beautiful Lady once more came down
from Heaven.

"Please, Mamma. Come with us tomorrow to the Cova to see Our
Lady."

"Our Lady! What childish nonsense! You are just being stubborn
and silly. Tomorrow we are all going to the celebrations for the feast of
St. Anthony. Don't you want to get your roll of bread . . . and hear the
bands . . . and see the great procession . . . and the firecrackers . . . and
be there for the wonderful sermon?"

Wasted words! But how could *she* understand? She forgot—no, actually she did not believe that she was speaking to a child whose eyes had beheld the Heavenly beauty of the Blessed Mother of God. Loaves of bread and bands and firecrackers! Such worldly attractions no longer held the slightest interest for her little seven-year-old daughter. For a month now, in reparation for sinners and to keep their promise to the Beautiful Lady, Jacinta and her two friends had given up the dancing which they once loved so much; had daily given away their lunches to the poor children they met along the way; and many times had made the sacrifice of doing without even a drink of water on those long hot days when they were parched with thirst from the merciless heat of the sun. Mother and child no longer spoke the same language.

"But, Mamma, Our Lady really did appear at the Cova."

"Nonsense, child. Our Lady certainly did not appear to *you*. It is just a useless waste of time to go there."

"No, Mamma. She really did. She told us she would come back on the thirteenth of the month and she will."

First thing next morning Jacinta hurried to her mother's room. She would ask her again to come to the Cova. But the room was empty. She awakened Francisco, and while he was dressing she let out the sheep. It was a disappointment to find her mother gone, but, she thought to herself, at least they could now go in peace to the Cova.

Lucy was already waiting for them. Hurt to the soul at the utter lack of understanding and violent opposition on the part of her own mother, she longed to be with her little companions who alone would understand. In later years, speaking of those early days, she wrote: "I recalled the times that were past and I kept asking myself what had become of the affection which my family had entertained for me only a short while before." Lucy, too, was experiencing *her* share of the suffering they had so readily offered to accept in reparation for the sins of men.

In due course they reached the Cova. In spite of the ridicule and unbelief that had greeted their story, there were about sixty curious onlookers,

Lucy's father among them. The children seated themselves in the shade of a large holm oak, and as time went on Lucy grew serious and apprehensive. Soon she was heard to exclaim: "Quiet, Our Lady is coming."

They began the recitation of the Rosary, but before it was finished she stood erect and shouted to Jacinta: "Our Lady is coming. I just saw the flash."

The three children ran to the smaller holm oak tree where the Lady had appeared in May, and while they knelt there Lucy was heard to say: "You told me to come today. What do you wish me to do?"

"I want you to come again on the thirteenth of next month. Now, when you say the Rosary, after each decade add the following prayer: 'Oh, my Jesus, forgive us our sins. Save us from the fire of Hell and lead all souls to Heaven, especially those who have most need of Thy Mercy.' "

The Blessed Lady then told Lucy that she wanted her to learn to read and write and promised that she would later tell her what else she wanted her to do. So overcome was the child by the beauty of the Heavenly Visitor that almost involuntarily she gave voice to her request that she take them all to Heaven. The answer of the Blessed Mother was significant.

"I will come soon and take Francisco and Jacinta. But you are to stay here for a longer time. God wishes to use you to make me known and loved, to establish throughout the world devotion to my Immaculate Heart. To all those who embrace it I promise salvation, and their souls will be loved by God as flowers placed by me before His throne."

Lucy was almost in tears. "Dear Lady," she cried, saddened at the thought of losing her little companions, "am I to stay here all alone?"

"No, my child. I will never leave you. If this thought causes you great sadness, remember that my Immaculate Heart will ever be your refuge and the way that will lead you to God."

As the Blessed Mother uttered these words she extended her hands, and in the rays of light that shone from them the children saw themselves as if submerged in the Divine Presence. Jacinta and Francisco were on the side of the light that was ascending to Heaven while Lucy was in the light that seemed to be diffused all over the earth. Before the palm of the Lady's right hand there was a heart, pierced by thorns, and the children understood that it was the Immaculate Heart of Mary, offended by the sins of a heedless world and pleading for reparation.

The crowd now saw Lucy rise to her feet and extend her hand toward the East. "There she goes," she cried. "There she goes."

The people saw only a white cloud rising slowly toward the East and noticed a movement in the branches of the oak tree. As Lucy announced that the Lady was going, these branches were brushed aside as if by an invisible hand and bent in the direction of the East. For a few minutes the children remained silent, their eyes riveted on the direction in which the Lady had disappeared. "There! It's over," cried Lucy. "She has entered Heaven and the doors are closed."

"It doesn't seem to me like a revelation from Heaven. It hardly seems possible that the Blessed Virgin would come down from Heaven just to tell you that the Rosary should be said every day. Already it is being said by nearly everybody in the parish. Ordinarily, when a thing like this happens, God directs the souls to whom he makes himself known to tell everything to their pastor or their confessor, but this child holds back as much as possible. It could be a trick of the devil. Time will tell us just what attitude we should adopt."

There it was, the verdict of the pastor as relayed to Lucy's mother, who had brought the frightened child for a final interview. They had been brought before him individually and all together, but they were so frightened that Jacinta maintained complete silence, Francisco mumbled only a few words, while Lucy gave a very sketchy and altogether unsatisfying account of what had happened. Had she said more, she might have set his doubts at rest. But now she was more frightened than ever.

A trick of the devil? Who was she to gainsay his words? Did she think she knew more than the priest? It was a very disturbed Lucy who wended her way home and there were very real doubts in her mind as to the authenticity of the apparitions. The thought became almost an obsession. She dreamed that the devil was laughing at her because he had deceived her so easily; that he was reaching out his claws to drag her into Hell. She began to feel sorry that she had ever become involved in the whole terrible affair, and the only place she knew any peace was in the presence of Jacinta and Francisco beside the little holm oak tree.

The day of the next apparition was drawing near. But Lucy had made her decision. She would go no more to the Cova da Iria. Her mother's repeated insistence that the pastor was right, that it was but a trick of the devil, had so confused and frightened the child that she was more disturbed than ever before. On July 12 she went to Francisco and Jacinta and told them of her decision.

"But *we* are going," Jacinta declared. "The Lady told us." On the verge of tears she told Lucy that if she were not there *they* would have to speak to the Lady. The thought was almost too much for the timid child.

But Lucy was adamant. "If the Lady asks for me," she cautioned, "tell her that I am not going because I am afraid she is the devil." Lucy herself was putting forth a brave front, but she burst into tears as she hurried away from her little companions.

The next morning, up to the very moment when it was time to leave for the Cova, Lucy experienced the same doubts and fears. But suddenly, as if a great dark cloud had passed from before her eyes and a great weight had been lifted from her soul, all her doubts vanished and her peace of mind returned. Joyfully now, and without any misgivings, she went to acquaint her little cousins of her change of mind. They were kneeling by the side of the bed, crying pitifully.

"Aren't you going to the Cova?" she asked them.

"We wouldn't dare go if you weren't there," they replied. And then, sensing that Lucy was going after all, they ran joyously from the house to join the throngs already on the way.

Ti Marto had long since made up his mind. The children were not lying. They never lied. He knew that all the accusations made against their families and against the clergy, who were accused of inventing the whole story, were patently false. God forgive him, but he felt that even the pastor was wrong, since he supposed the visions were the work of the devil. Right now he was slowly making his way through a throng of some five thousand villagers, and it was with great difficulty that he finally managed to get to the holm oak and stand beside his little Jacinta.

Once again, as they were nearing the end of the Rosary, Lucy looked toward the East and cried to the crowd: "Close your umbrellas. Our Lady is coming." There was the same brilliant flash of light, this time engulfing the three children, and there again was the beautiful Lady, her eyes resting lovingly on Lucy, as if in acknowledgment of the suffering the child had been called upon to endure in her behalf.

"I want you to come here again, on the thirteenth of next month," she said. "Continue to say the Rosary every day in honor of Our Lady of the Rosary to obtain the peace of the world and the end of the war, for she alone will be able to help."

Here, thought Lucy, was the opportunity to set all her doubts at rest. Here, in the very presence of the lovely Lady, she could find out once and for all if this was but a trick of the devil or really an apparition from Heaven. "Dear Lady, will you please tell us who you are? Will you work a miracle so that all the people will know that you really do appear to us?"

"Continue to come every month," the Lady replied. "In October I will tell you who I am and will work a miracle so great that all will believe in the reality of the apparitions."

Even as she said these words, the Lady once again opened her hands and the rays of light that shone from them seemed to pierce the very heart of the earth. The children looked—but the earth was no longer there.

They were gazing into a veritable ocean of fire. "Even the earth itself seemed to vanish, and we saw huge numbers of devils and lost souls in a vast and fiery ocean. The devils resembled black animals, hideous and unknown, each filling the air with despairing shrieks. The lost souls were in their human bodies and seemed brown in color, tumbling about constantly in the flames and screaming with terror. All were on fire, within and without their bodies, and neither devils nor damned souls seemed able to control their movements. They were tossing about like coals in a fiery furnace, with never an instant's peace or freedom from pain."

So terrible was this awful vision that Lucy later declared that they would have died of fright, were it not for the fact that the Blessed Lady was standing beside them and had already assured them that they would go to Heaven. Now deathly pale, they looked toward the Blessed Mother.

"You have seen Hell," she explained to them, "where the souls of sinners go. To save them God wishes to establish in the world the devotion to my Immaculate Heart. If people do as I shall ask, many souls will be converted and there will be peace. This war is going to end, but if people do not cease offending God, not much time will elapse and during the Pontificate of Pius XI another and more terrible war will begin. When you shall see a night illumined by an unknown light, know that this is the great sign from God that the chastisement of the world for its many transgressions is at hand through war, famine, persecution of the Church and of the Holy Father.

"To prevent this, I shall come to ask for the consecration of Russia to my Immaculate Heart and the Communion of reparation on the First Saturdays. If my requests are heard, Russia will be converted and there will be peace. If not, she will spread her errors throughout the entire world, provoking wars and persecution of the Church. The good will suffer martyrdom; the Holy Father will suffer much; different nations will be annihilated. But in the end my Immaculate Heart will triumph.

The Holy Father will consecrate Russia to me, and it will be converted and some time of peace will be granted to humanity."[2]

Still overcome by the terrible vision of Hell and anxious to make any sacrifice demanded by the Blessed Lady, Lucy turned and asked her: "Is there anything else you want me to do?"

"No, today I desire nothing else from you."

There was a sudden sound as of thunder. "There she goes," Lucy shouted. "There she goes." With a last affectionate glance in the direction of her little ones the Lady glided slowly toward the East and "disappeared in the immense distance of the firmament."

The publicity resulting from the newspaper discussions of the "supposed" apparitions and word of the harsh treatment meted out to the children by both their own families and the civil authorities had aroused the local people to a feverish pitch of curiosity. At the Cova on August 13 there were nearly 18,000 present, the majority of whom were devout believers. While awaiting the arrival of the children they prayed, sang, and said the Rosary. But on this occasion the children did not appear. The Administrator had seen to that. They were imprisoned in his own house. Murmurs of indignation began to swell among the disappointed throng. Many urged that they go and lodge a strong protest with the authorities. But while they were discussing the matter something happened that at once disarmed and consoled them and convinced them more strongly than ever that this was, indeed, a visitation from Heaven. From out the clear blue sky there suddenly came the rumble of heavy thunder and a vividly brilliant flash of lightning. The sun grew pale and the whole atmosphere changed to a dull, sickly sort of yellow, while a light cloud,

---

[2] It was not until 1927 that Lucy was permitted to reveal the two parts of this great secret, the vision of Hell and the necessity of devotion to the Immaculate Heart of Mary. The third part, written and sealed in the archives of the Bishop of Leiria, was not to be made known until 1960, though would not necessarily be made known even then. Actually, the bishop decided not to reveal the secret.

of beautiful shape, appeared and hovered a while over the oak tree and the place of the apparitions. Filled with awe at this manifestation which they took to mean an expression of displeasure on the part of the Heavenly Lady, they calmly dispersed and went peacefully to their homes.

The children's imprisonment continued for another three days, during which time the Administrator had recourse to all sorts of threats to make them contradict one another or to disclose the great secret confided to them. His efforts were unavailing. Finally, in desperation, realizing that he was getting nowhere and that there was every danger that the affair might get completely out of hand, he said angrily to the children: "Either you tell me the truth or I shall have you fried alive in a red-hot frying pan."

One by one he led the children away as if he were going to carry out his threat. Lucy was the last to be taken, and when later she was asked how she felt about it she confided: "I surely thought that he meant what he said and that I was going to die in the pan, but I could not betray my secret and I placed myself in the hands of Our Lady." Remarkable fortitude on the part of little children! Reminiscent of the courage of the martyrs of old, whom neither rack nor rope nor consuming fire could force to betray their God.

The Administrator was beaten. He was obliged to take the children back to the parish priest on August 16, three days after they were to have appeared at the Cova. The pastor brought them home to their anxious parents, who had heard all sorts of rumors as to the fate that had befallen them.

Having thus been prevented by force from keeping their appointment at the Cova, the children went back to their ordinary occupations. On the nineteenth of August they were keeping watch over the flock at a place called Valinhos when suddenly the Lady appeared. She complained about the actions of the Administrator and said that because of this interference the miracle announced for October would be less striking than it otherwise would have been. Little is recorded of the conversations during this apparition, but once more, as at Lourdes to Bernadette, the Blessed Mother spoke earnestly of the dire necessity of penance, both for one's own transgressions and those of a sinful world. She told them that many souls were lost forever because there was nobody to make sacrifices and to pray for them.

The children brought home part of the branch on which the Lady had rested her foot, and while Lucy's mother was examining it a fragrant and delicate perfume, of a kind utterly unknown in the area, emanated from the foliage surrounding it. Lucy's mother was by now convinced of the genuineness of the apparitions, and she felt a real remorse for the harsh treatment she had meted out to her daughter when first she heard their story.

By now no restrictions or prohibitions on the part of the local authorities could avail to keep the pious pilgrims away from the little Cova, already beginning to be venerated as a shrine. On September 13 there were 30,000 people present before the arrival of the children, and throughout the whole assembly were little groups reciting the Rosary with a reverence and an emotion such as they had never known before. Precisely at noon the kneeling throng saw the sun grow dim and the atmosphere take on the color of dull gold. Suddenly, not from the children this time but from the crowd itself, cries of surprise and joy broke out from end to end of that vast assembly.

"There she is. . . . Over there . . . look . . . she's coming . . . she's coming."

In the cloudless sky a luminous globe had suddenly appeared before the eyes of the astonished crowd. Moving from East to West, it glided slowly and majestically across the heavens while a light white cloud enveloped the oak tree and the children. More wonderful still, while the globe still moved and the three children remained hidden behind the cloud a great shower of white roses suddenly fell from the heavens, reached almost to the earth, and then dissolved from sight. In awe the crowd listened to Lucy's voice as she conversed with the invisible Lady. Once again she stressed the necessity of reciting the Rosary to bring the war to an end.

And now she divulged for the first time some details of the great miracle to take place in October. She told the children that on that occasion both the Child Jesus and St. Joseph would be with her. To Lucy's request that she cure the sick, the Lady replied:

"I will cure some of them but not all, because the Lord has no confidence in them."

It seemed that all Portugal knew it by now. The Blessed Mother had promised a miracle for October, a miracle so great that all would believe in the reality of the apparitions. Tension mounted as the great day drew near, the vast majority of devout believers waiting eagerly for her to keep her promise and confound the enemies of God, the atheists and scoffers welcoming the impending "showdown," the anti-climax that once and for all would give the lie to this whole sorry business. From the farthest corners of Portugal, pilgrims were converging upon Fatima on the days preceding the time of the hoped-for miracle. We are indebted to Dr. William Thomas Walsh, in his book, *Our Lady of Fatima*, for a most vivid description of the plight of these thousands of people during the terrible, never-to-be-forgotten night of the twelfth of October, 1917.

It was as if the devil, somewhere in the ice and snow that could never slake the burning of his pain, had resolved to destroy with one blow all that remained of the Europe which had so long been his battleground against the Thing he hated most. Somewhere in the dark misery of Siberia, he was permitted, heaven knows why, to disturb the equilibrium of the air, setting in motion a cold and cutting blast that shrieked across the continent to the western sea. It may have passed howling over a cabin in Finland where a little lynx-eyed man who called himself Lenin was waiting to enter St. Petersburg . . . and to begin, in a very few weeks, the transformation and destruction of all that world which owed what was best and noblest in it to the teachings of Christ. . . . It scourged poor wretches of both armies into the cover of slimy dugouts all along the western front, and plastered with mud the Italian fugitives from Caporetto. It seemed to echo and enlarge the despair that was settling over the vineyards of war-wearied France, where Haig stood, as he said, with his back to the wall. Finally it dashed itself against the Pyrenees, and then, as if it had gathered up all the hatreds and discontents of disobedient men and all the rebellious powers of a corrupted nature in its mad career from the Baltic to Cape Saint Vincent, it let them all loose on the little country that has never been permanently conquered, the land where she who treads upon the serpent's head has long been honored, the *terra da Santa Maria.*

It was during this night, when the very furies of Hell seemed loosed upon humanity, that tens of thousands of people, some of them traveling for days and nights already, converged from every part of Portugal upon the little Cova da Iria. We continue from *Our Lady of Fatima:*

Peasant families slung their wicker baskets and earthen water jugs over their shoulders, or packed them in panniers on the backs of burros, and started out under the lowering skies. Fathers and mothers carried sick and lame children in their arms for incredible distances. Fishermen left their nets and boats on the beaches of the Vieira and took to the oozy roads. Farmhands from Monte Real, sailors from ships in the harbors of Porto or Algarve, factory workers from Lisboa, *serranas* from Minde or Soublio, ladies and gentlemen, scrubwomen, waiters, young and old, rich and poor, all sorts of people (but most of them humble, most of them barefoot, most of them workers and their families) were plodding through the mud under the pelting rain that night, like a great scattered army converging upon Fatima, hoping to find there some favor of health or conversion, forgiveness of sin, consolation for sorrow, the beginning of a better life, the blessing of the Mother of God.

Morning dawned. The fury of the storm had somewhat abated, but the merciless rain still fell and every road in the area was by now a veritable quagmire. Word had gotten round that some of the belabored pilgrims were in an extremely ugly mood. There had better be a miracle, they said. For it was the promise of those children that had sent them battling through the unforgettable ordeal of last night's journey and Heaven help them if this turned out to be a fiasco. The children and their families had already been alerted to the danger. Jacinta's mother was especially concerned. She prayed more fervently than usual that day. She was amazed that her children should be so serenely unafraid.

"If they hurt us," said Jacinta, "we will go to Heaven. But those that hurt us, poor people, will go to Hell."

It was a long, tedious journey to the Cova. The narrow road was clogged with weary travelers, and as Ti Marto tried to make way for the children, men and women dropped to their knees in the slimy mud, imploring their prayers or surged even closer to see or if possible to touch the "little saints" who had been told that they would all go to Heaven.

When finally they reached the scene of the apparitions they looked out over a human sea of pilgrims, a dark mass of humanity under their rain-soaked blankets or wilting sombreros or black umbrellas that seemed to cover the countryside. A priest who had spent the night in the mud and rain was standing near the holm oak tree. Alternately he read from his breviary and glanced nervously at his watch. "At what hour," he asked, "will the Lady appear?"

"At noon," Lucy replied.

"But it is already noon," he answered. "Our Lady is not a liar."

Minutes passed. He glanced at his watch again. "It is past noon. Away with all this. It is only an illusion."

Murmurs of impatience and disappointment were being heard among the crowd. But suddenly Lucy exclaimed: "Kneel down, Jacinta, for now I see Our Lady."

There it was, the familiar flash that heralded the appearance of the Heavenly visitor. The faces of the children assumed an ecstatic expression, and once more the bystanders realized that they were gazing at the beautiful Lady. The interview was brief. The Lady kept her promise to tell them who she was. She announced:

"I am the Lady of the Rosary."

Her face grew grave as she imparted her last message to the children. "People must amend their lives, ask pardon for their sins, and not offend Our Lord any more for He is already too greatly offended."

As she took her leave of the children she opened her hands, and from them rays of light extended in the direction of the sun. "There she goes! There she goes!" shouted Lucy and her words found echo in a great cry of astonishment from the multitude, by now observing the first awe-inspiring manifestations of the Miracle of the Sun.

Gradually the sun grew pale, lost its normal color, and appeared as a silver disk at which all could gaze directly without even shading their eyes. Then, to the astonishment of all present, rays of multicolored light shot out in every direction; red, blue, yellow, green—every color of the spectrum. Meanwhile, the very heavens seemed to be revolving as the sun spun madly on its axis like a gigantic wheel of fire, painting the rocks, the trees, the faces of the people with sunshine such as human eye had never seen before. Three times it stopped and three times the mad dance was resumed. Then, while the crowd went to its knees in abject terror, the sun suddenly seemed to be torn loose from its place in the heavens. Down it hurtled, closer and closer to earth, staggering "drunkenly" as it zigzagged through the skies while from all parts of the now terrified multitude arose cries of repentance and appeals for mercy.

"It's the end of the world," shrieked one woman hysterically.

"Dear God, don't let me die in my sins," cried another.

"Holy Virgin, protect us," implored a third.

Suddenly, as if arrested in its downward plunge by an invisible Heavenly hand, it poised for a moment and then, in the same series of swirling motions it began to climb upward till it resumed its accustomed place in the heavens. Gone was the silver disk with the brilliant rays. It was once more a ball of fire at which nobody could look directly with unshaded eyes.

While people looked at one another, still trembling from their terrifying experience and not yet sure that some further disaster would not overtake them, a cry of astonishment was heard on every side. Their rain-sodden garments had suddenly dried and everybody felt comfortable and warm. It was a gracious maternal gesture on the part of the Blessed Mother, in the wake of the greatest miracle our generation has ever known.

Meanwhile, the children had been permitted to behold a vision of the Holy Family in a series of Heavenly tableaux. First there was Our Lord, as a grown man, dressed in red and blessing the multitude. Then he appeared as an infant, with St. Joseph and His Blessed Mother, and finally the Blessed Virgin appeared in the brown robes of Our Lady of Mount Carmel. The first and last visions were seen by Lucy alone, Francisco and Jacinta being privileged to witness only the apparition of the Holy Family. It was, indeed, of special significance for Lucy, who was later to become a Carmelite Sister in the convent of Coimbra after fulfilling her Heaven-sent assignment of giving to the world the urgent message of the necessity of devotion to the Immaculate Heart.

It was in response to Lucy's request—"Please take us all to Heaven"—that the Blessed Mother made it known that she would come *soon* to take Francisco and Jacinta. The fulfillment of that promise was not to be long delayed. It was October 1918, just one year after the final apparition. Throughout the entire world the greatest influenza epidemic ever known was taking its terrible toll of lives, and not even the remote little village of Fatima was immune from its depredations. Hardly a day but saw a black-robed cortege of mourners winding their way to the village church and cemetery.

Francisco was the first of the Marto family to fall victim to the dread disease, and it was with breaking hearts that his father and mother saw the child welcome the fatal illness as the beginning of the fulfillment of the Lady's promise to take him soon to Heaven. The story of his latter days on earth, of his cheerful acceptance of every suffering and sacrifice "in reparation for sin and for the conversion of sinners," is one of the most moving and inspiring chapters of the whole narrative of Fatima. Nothing in this world any longer held the slightest attraction for this ten-year-old child "on the threshold of Heaven," and his one consuming desire, born of a spiritual perception far beyond his tender years, was "to console the good God" for the heedless ingratitude of so many millions throughout a sinful world.

"Which do you like better," Lucy asked him one day, "to console Our Lord or to convert sinners so that their souls won't go to Hell?"

The theological implications of this profound question were probably not realized by Lucy, but with a love approaching the heights of spiritual perfection Francisco answered without hesitation: "I'd rather console Our Lord."

"But don't you remember how sad Our Lady was when she said not to offend Our Lord any more because He was already too much offended?"

"I want first to console Our Lord and then convert the sinners so that they will not offend Him any more."

Francisco rallied appreciably after the initial ravages of the influenza. He even became well enough to visit the Cabeço cave of the Angel and the little holm oak, hallowed by the repeated visits of the Lady from Heaven. For hours at a time he would remain prostrate on the ground, now lost in heavenly contemplation, now reciting over and over the prayer of the Angel. Returning to the little village, the child would make his way to church and there, in the presence of his hidden Lord, would remain for hours on his knees. Who can fathom the depths of the heavenly secrets vouchsafed to this victim soul, a humble illiterate child, one of the weak chosen by God to confound the strong because no flesh may glory in His sight!

Before the end of January, Francisco was ill once more. From now on he could not leave his bed, and by the first of April he was so weak that he could hardly utter a single prayer. His great desire was to receive his first Communion, and the priest was to come to him that night. He asked a special favor of his parents. Could Lucy and Jacinta come to see him, and could he speak to them alone?

"I am going to confession," he told them when everybody else had left the room. "I am going to receive Holy Communion, and then I am going to die. I want you, Lucy, to tell me if you have ever seen me commit any sin. And I want Jacinta to tell me too."

The children racked their memories. There was that time when he had joined the boys of Aljustrel in throwing stones at the rival "gang" from Boleiros. And once, a long time ago, he had taken a *tostão* from his father to buy a hand organ from José Marto of Casa Velha.

"I've already confessed those sins," he told them. "But I will confess them again. Perhaps it is for these sins of mine that Our Lord is so sad." And joining his hands fervently he recited the prayer told them by the Lady: "Oh, my Jesus, forgive us our sins. Save us from the fire of Hell and lead all souls to Heaven, especially those who have most need of your mercy."

It was the morning of April 3, 1919, when Francisco received his first Communion. One day later, ten o'clock on the morning of April 4, the Lady came and her promise was fulfilled.

While the thought of consoling the good God had been the perpetual preoccupation of Francisco, it was the terrible vision of Hell that haunted little Jacinta during her remaining days on earth. She could never dismiss it from her mind. Over and over she would ask Lucy if she remembered the frightening things they had seen; all those people screaming in terror and burning like sticks of wood in a fire and never, never to know any alleviation of their eternal agony. At times the thought was almost more than the child could bear.

"Lucy," she asked one day, "why doesn't the Lady show Hell to everybody? Then nobody would ever again commit a mortal sin. "

Jacinta had fallen ill shortly after Francisco, but she recovered rapidly and her happy parents assured her that she was now really out of danger. But the child knew. She would never be well again. The Blessed Mother had revealed to her that she was going to two hospitals and that in the second one—which would be very dark—she was going to die all alone.

The influenza returned. And as in the case of Francisco, it proved to be more devastating than ever. One morning in July 1919, Ti Marto placed the child on the back of a burro and brought her to the hospital at Ourem. It was a large, white, cheerful building, and she realized at once that this was not "the dark place" where the Lady had told her she was going to die. Jacinta had long been undergoing severe suffering. An incision had been made and a drain inserted in her side, but after two months it was obvious to all concerned that her life was slowly wasting away. The daily dressings of the wound caused her excruciating pain, and Doctor Formigao, who saw her in October, described her as "a living skeleton, her arms nothing but bones, her face all eyes, her cheeks wasted away by fever."

On February 2, 1920, Jacinta was taken to the Hospital of Dona Stefania in Lisbon. It was a gloomy, cheerless, depressing sort of building, and this, she felt, was the dark place. Here she would die all alone. After a thorough examination the chief surgeon confirmed the previous diagnosis of purulent pleurisy and announced that as soon as her strength returned an operation would be performed.

"But, doctor," she remonstrated, "it will do no good. Our Lady has come to tell me that I am going to die soon."

The operation was duly performed. She was so weak that it was necessary to administer a local anesthetic. Two ribs were removed, and during the terrible pain of the operation the child was heard to repeat Our Lady's name over and over. Then she would murmur weakly: "Patience. We should suffer everything to go to Heaven . . . Now you can convert many souls, my dear Jesus, because I suffer so much for You."

For six days the excruciating pains continued, but on the night of February 16 she told her nurse that she had again seen Our Lady. "She said that she was coming for me very soon and would take away all my pain." From then on she suffered no more. On the evening of February 20 she called her nurse, told her she was about to die, and asked for the Last Sacraments. Shortly afterward she made her confession to Father Periera dos Reis, who promised that he would bring her Holy Communion in the morning.

"But I am going to die, Father, this very night." Jacinta pleaded earnestly that he bring her holy Viaticum that evening, but the good padre did not take seriously her conviction of imminent death. It was at ten-thirty "that very night" that she breathed her last, a smile upon her lips as if in greeting to the beautiful Lady whose arms had opened to enfold her in Heavenly embrace.

Lucy was by now the object of great curiosity among her own people and among those who came from far and near. Even in her own home she found no escape, and her mother's utter lack of sympathy only made the situation more difficult to endure. While Francisco and Jacinta had lived she could always go to them, assured of that sympathy and understanding that was their common heritage as sharers of the precious heavenly secret. But now Francisco and Jacinta were gone. And soon she herself was to say good-by to her familiar fields, her little flocks of sheep, and the Cova, hallowed by the repeated visits of the Lady from Heaven. It was decided by the bishop that Lucy, if only for her own sake, was to be taken away from Fatima. She would be sent to Porto where there was a girls' school conducted by the Sisters of St. Dorothy. All the preliminaries were to be arranged with the utmost secrecy. Nobody but her mother was to know that she was going away, and when she did arrive at the boarding school she was to maintain strict silence as to her identity and whatever pertained to the Fatima apparitions. Two o'clock on the morning of May 16, 1921, was the hour set for the departure. She was accompanied by her mother and an uncle, and at the Cova they entered the chapel of the apparitions, built in 1917, and together recited the Rosary. At Leiria mother and child, both in tears, bade each other farewell. In the company of a friendly lady Lucy was to continue her journey. Nevermore, she believed, was she to see her childhood home or the hallowed spots so dear to her heart and soul.[3]

When Lucy arrived at the Asilo de Vilar school in Porto she was the object of great interest on the part of the Community who viewed her with mixed curiosity and suspicion. Her technical and social education went on apace, but in the more sophisticated and academic atmosphere there was little of sympathy or maternal understanding. In his book, *Our Lady of Fatima*, Archbishop Ryan speaks of this difficult period of readjustment: "It is to be supposed, of course," he writes, "that exercises of religion were prominent in the day's routine but anything like recognition of the child's possible starvation for spiritual sympathy was vetoed by the ruling that any reference to Fatima was

---

[3] Once more, before entering Carmel and shutting out the world forever, Lucy, then a Sister of St. Dorothy, was permitted to revisit Fatima. To Father Galamba, who accompanied her, she showed the place of the apparition of the Angel, and when they stopped before the graves of Francisco and Jacinta she broke down and cried as if her heart would break. Twenty-nine years had passed, and the humble little place of the apparitions had now become a world-famous shrine.

taboo." In her heart of hearts how little Lucy must have longed for the carefree days at the Cova and the companionship of her little confidants wherein there was always such mutual and happy understanding. But in a spirit of true obedience and willing self-denial she cheerfully accepted this trial. Like her dear departed little companions, she had long since learned to welcome every sort of sacrifice and penance, to be offered up for poor sinners and in reparation to the Immaculate Heart of Mary.

In November 1926, Lucy entered the novitiate of the Sisters of St. Dorothy. She made her first vows in November 1928 and her final profession in 1934. For nearly fourteen years she exerted every possible effort to spread further the devotion to the Immaculate Heart of Mary, and it was not till March 1948 that she felt free to devote the rest of her life to her own spiritual perfection. It must have been a blessed relief when she entered the Carmelite Order at Coimbra with the realization that nevermore would she be plagued by the importunities of curious visitors who were dying to know, among other things, if the Blessed Mother wore earrings or used perfume.

Forty-two years have elapsed since the Blessed Mother gave us her "Peace Plan from Heaven." She tried to stem the flood of moral evil that led to the Second World War and the spread of Communism throughout the world. Contemporary history bears witness to the fact that her efforts ended in failure. Listen to her prophetic words of solemn warning spoken in July 1917 and consider in what a welter of human agony the threatened calamities have come to pass: "If people do as I shall ask, many souls will be converted and there will be peace. This war is going to end, but if people do not cease offending God, not much time will elapse and during the Pontificate of Pius XI another and more terrible war will begin . . . If my requests are heard, Russia will be converted and there will be peace. If not, she will spread her errors throughout the entire world, provoking wars and persecution of the Church. The good will suffer martyrdom; the Holy Father will suffer much; different nations will be annihilated. . . ."

But the picture is not hopeless. We are assured of the final and inevitable triumph. ". . . in the end my Immaculate Heart will triumph. The Holy Father will consecrate Russia to me, and it will be converted and some time of peace will be granted to humanity."

It still rests with Mary's own children to avert appalling disaster for the world before that consummation so devoutly to be desired. Her diagnosis of the cause of such disaster is as true today as when she flashed out of the skies of Heaven in 1917. The cause is revolt against God, and today that revolt is fast assuming the proportions of universal apostasy. There are many who believe that the situation is now out of human hands; that we have passed the point of no return; that only direct Divine intervention can now resolve the terrible impasse. Such intervention may truly be apocalyptic, and it is in the Hands of God to permit—or to prevent—nuclear war that could wipe out civilization or world Communism that would mean universal slavery and martyrdom. "The Hand of my Son in Heaven is now so heavy that I cannot hold it back any longer." Thus spoke the Mother of God when she knew that Europe was doomed. Fidelity to the message of Fatima; daily recitation of the Rosary; a serious determined effort at personal sanctity; the devotion of the First Saturdays and consecration to her Immaculate Heart; this, on the part of her own children may still lighten the Hand of God and strengthen the arm of our Blessed Mother as she tries to save us from "suffering such as humankind has never known before."

We shall be wise indeed if we learn the lesson of the children of Fatima.

BEAURAING

1932–33

THE VIRGIN WITH THE GOLDEN HEART

Don Sharkey

Our Lady had said at Fatima, in 1917, that if men did not stop offending her Son the world would be punished by means of wars, famines, and persecutions of the Church. These things were already under way in 1932 when Mary made the first of her thirty-three appearances in Beauraing, Belgium. The Communists were in power in Russia and were trying to extend their godless rule throughout the world. Benito Mussolini was master of Italy and was persecuting the Church and was following a course which would soon lead to disaster. Adolf Hitler was rising in Germany and would assume complete power within a few months. Communists, Fascists, and Nazis were all aided by the unrest caused by the world-wide depression. The end of 1932 and the beginning of 1933 were a time of widespread unemployment, of bread lines, of hunger, and of bloody riots.

It was a troubled world in which Our Lady appeared in 1932 and a world which had even greater troubles in store for it. The warnings had been given at Fatima. Apparently the time for warnings was past, and so Our Lady came as a Merciful Mother—a messenger of hope.

Beauraing is a village of about 2000 people in the Walloon, or French-speaking, part of Belgium. This section comprises roughly the southern half of the little country. (In the northern half, Flanders, the people speak Flemish, which is similar to Dutch.) The Blessed Virgin was to speak French in her apparitions.

Beauraing is sixty miles southeast of Brussels, the capital of Belgium. It is twelve miles from the city of Dinant and two or three miles from the French border. Most of the people of the region make their living by farming, and some work in the nearby quarries and forests. Those who do not own farms have large gardens. In 1932 the effects of the depression were softened in Beauraing and similar rural villages by the fact that the people had farms and gardens to keep them in food and to keep them occupied.

At one time the people of the region had been staunch Catholics, but by 1932 many of them had drifted away from the Church. Some were merely indifferent toward the Catholic faith; others were hostile to it. The Labor party, which is Marxist and anti-Catholic, carried the district in many elections.

Gilberte Voisin, a thirteen-year-old girl of Beauraing, attended the Academy conducted by the Sisters of Christian Doctrine. She was a semi-boarder at the school. This means that she did not go home when afternoon classes were over as did the day students, but neither did she stay all night as did the boarders. She stayed at the school for an afternoon meal and for a study period and then left for home about 6:30 P.M. Gilberte was an alert, clear-minded girl with a round pink face, deep dimples, brown mischievous eyes, and chestnut brown hair. She was of a rather religious nature and belonged to the Eucharistic Crusade.

In the past, Gilberte's father had gone to the school to walk home with her, but lately he had been sending her brother and sister for her. They loved this task and begged to be allowed to go for Gilberte.

Gilberte's parents, Mr. and Mrs. Hector Voisin, were typical of thousands of Walloons who did not live up to the tenets of their religion. Neither had attended Mass or received the sacraments in many years. They had sent their other two children to the state schools. "It was only because of her health," Hector Voisin was to say later, "that we decided to send Gilberte to the Academy. This child had no appetite, and we knew that the Sisters know how to make the children eat." Gilberte had long been praying that her parents would return to the Church.

Hector Voisin, at the end of 1932, was forty-one years old. He was of medium height and had black hair, a small mustache, and dark piercing eyes. He was assistant manager of the railroad station and painted houses in his spare time. His wife, Marie Louise, was thirty-eight, blond, and rather plump. She was sociable and friendly, a good housekeeper and a good mother. She ran the little shop which the Voisins had in the front of their house and which carried a stock of wallpaper, paint, linoleum, and similar items.

On the evening of November 29, 1932, Fernande and Albert Voisin started toward the Academy to walk home with their sister. Fernande was fifteen and a half and looked younger. She was small and had brown eyes, black hair, and olive-colored skin. She had a pleasing smile and a gentle disposition. Albert, eleven, was also small for his age, had an oval face, large sparkling blue eyes, and lips that seemed always about to break into a laugh.

On their way to the Academy, Fernande and Albert passed the home of the Degeimbre family. They rapped at the kitchen shutters and in a few moments were joined by two of the Degeimbre girls, Andree and

Gilberte. Andree was fourteen and looked to be about sixteen. She was blond, shy, somewhat slow in speech. Gilberte Degeimbre was nine and had blond hair and eyes of azure blue. She was in turn remarkably grave and gaily exuberant. She was an honest, straightforward girl, and one of her teachers said she believed Gilberte was incapable of telling a lie.

These two Degeimbre girls lived with their widowed mother, Germaine, and with their older sister, Jeanne. Mrs. Degeimbre was thirty-five years old, of medium height, had dark hair, and dark brown eyes. She looked like the sturdy, strong farm woman she was. She and her husband had managed a farm until his death, and now Mrs. Degeimbre and her three daughters had a small farm within the village of Beauraing. Mrs. Degeimbre was considered a practical Catholic although she made no great show of her religion and did not hesitate to miss Sunday Mass for reasons she considered sufficient.

Those are the five children and their parents. Two of the girls were named Gilberte. Both Gilbertes were students at the Academy, but Gilberte Degeimbre was a day student and went home in the afternoon. Despite the differences in their ages, the two girls were good friends. To distinguish them, people called the Voisin girl "Big Gilberte" and the Degeimbre girl "Little Gilberte."

Albert was the only boy among the five. Despite the fact that he was the second youngest of the group, he was the ringleader when it came to mischief. He rang five doorbells on the way to the Academy that night. Each time, the girls joined him in flight.

After the children had alternately walked and run a short distance from the Degeimbre home, they arrived at the convent where the school was located. Just past the convent the street was crossed by a high railroad viaduct. The railroad embankment ran behind the convent and grounds. The convent grounds were on the right hand of the street as the children faced the embankment. An iron fence surmounting a low stone wall separated the convent garden from the cobblestone street.

Behind the garden and facing the street was the large brick building which housed both the sisters' convent and the Academy.

The children walked through the big central gate into the garden, made a slight detour to visit a Lourdes grotto which stood in front of the railroad embankment, and then made their way up the gravel path to the front of the convent. They climbed the few steps that led to the front door and rang the doorbell. As they waited for the Sister portress to answer the bell, Albert turned and looked in the direction of the viaduct about fifty yards away.

"Look!" Albert cried. "The Blessed Virgin, dressed in white, is walking above the bridge!"

At first the girls thought that Albert was up to his usual mischief, but when they saw the expression of wonder on his face, they turned. Above the grotto and viaduct they saw the luminous figure of a lady in white. She was walking in the air. Through the folds of the lady's robe, they could see the movements of her knees as she walked. Her feet were hidden by a little cloud.

Frightened, the children rang the doorbell insistently and pounded on the door. Sister Valeria opened the door without noticing the children's excitement. She went to get Gilberte Voisin. Then while she was waiting for Gilberte to put on her coat she noticed through the partly opened door that the children were greatly agitated. She went to see what was the matter.

"Look, Sister, the Virgin is walking above the grotto."

But Sister could see nothing.

Then Gilberte Voisin came to the door, and she, too, saw the Lady.

"Oh!" she exclaimed.

The frightened children ran down the garden path to the street and then on to the Degeimbre home. Mrs. Degeimbre would not believe that the children had seen the Blessed Virgin. The three Voisin children went on to their home, and their parents would not believe them either.

The next evening the four children once more set out to meet Gilberte Voisin at the school. Their parents, thinking that the children had imagined the whole thing, readily permitted them to do so. They were sure that the children would see nothing and that this would be the end of the matter.

Gilberte came to the door of the convent, and the five children walked along the center path of the garden toward the gate. Then suddenly they saw the Lady again. She was walking over the railroad viaduct as she had the night before.

The children ran into Mrs. Degeimbre's house shouting: "We've seen her! It *is* the Blessed Virgin, and she is so much more beautiful than any of her statues!"

Mrs. Degeimbre was furious. She decided that someone was playing a practical joke on the children, and she was determined to expose the trickster. Mrs. Degeimbre had been left a widow about a year before and felt a double responsibility toward her daughters. The next evening, December 1, she and a group of friends and neighbors followed the four children when they went to the convent. Mrs. Degeimbre was armed with a stout stick.

The children were still out on the street when they saw the Lady standing on the center walk of the garden. She disappeared almost immediately.

Mrs. Degeimbre, who could see nothing, sent the four children to get Gilberte Voisin. Then, with her stick, she thrashed about in the bushes for the person who was playing tricks on her daughters. The other adults joined in the search.

Suddenly the adults heard cries of "Oh, oh" from the children. Gilberte Voisin had scarcely come out of the building and closed the door behind her when the Lady had appeared again. This time she was halfway between the front door and the Lourdes grotto. Her hands were joined; her eyes were raised to heaven. She lowered her eyes, smiled at the children, and disappeared.

Before the children got through the gate they saw the Lady for the third time that evening. By this time the children were interspersed among the adults, but the adults saw nothing. The Lady seemed to be coming out of the shrubs between the gate and the grotto. She rose toward heaven and disappeared.

Little Gilberte Degeimbre, the youngest of the five, was so overcome by the beauty of the apparition that she had to be taken home. Big Gilberte stayed with her while the other three children went back to the convent. This time all three parents went along. Before they had entered the gate the children shouted: "There she is!" They fell to their knees as if they had been struck down.

In high-pitched voices they prayed: "Hail Mary, full of grace, the Lord is with thee. . . ."

They were all looking at a hawthorn tree which was inside the garden, about ten feet from the fence, and to the left of the center walk. The Lady was appearing beneath an arched branch of this tree.

The Lady looked young, about eighteen or twenty; her smile lighted up her features. Her eyes were a beautiful deep blue. Rays of light came from her head. She wore a long, white, heavily pleated gown without a belt. The children said that the dress reflected a kind of blue light. She held her hands together, as if in prayer, during most of the apparition but parted them just before she disappeared, "like the priest at the *Dominus vobiscum.*"

She had no rosary during this apparition but later she would have one on her right arm.

This was the fourth vision of December 1 and the sixth vision the children had seen. This sixth vision set the pattern for those to come. Henceforth, the Lady would always appear beneath the arched branch of the hawthorn tree; the children would always be thrown to their knees when the Lady appeared, and they would always pray in high-pitched voices far different from their natural voices.

That evening the two mothers consulted Father Leon Lambert, their pastor and dean. He listened to the story in silence and advised them not to talk to anyone about the matter. It was difficult to heed this advice, because almost everyone in the village was talking about the apparitions.

The next day, December 2, Mother Theophile, the superior of the convent, decided to put an end to "this farce." She ordered the garden gates locked at dusk and two fierce dogs put in the yard. This did not keep the Lady from appearing to the children as they knelt on the cobblestones outside the garden.

Albert made himself the spokesman for the group and asked: "Are you the Immaculate Virgin?"

The Lady smiled and nodded her head.

"What do you want?" Albert asked.

Then came the first words uttered by Our Lady at Beauraing.

"Always be good."

She appeared two more times that day. During the third appearance she asked: "Is it true you will always be good?"

"Yes!" Andree cried. "We will always be good."

Then the Virgin disappeared.

On Saturday, December 3, the children stayed away from the garden, in obedience to Mother Theophile. They were sad because they would not see their Lady that day. At dusk when Mother Theophile went out to lock the garden gate, she found a crowd of 150 persons in the street.

"You are wasting your time here," Mother Theophile said. "There is nothing to see."

"What a Socialist we have in this woman," said a member of the crowd. "She has less belief in this business than we have."

The next day Mother Theophile relented. She said that because the children had obeyed her they could again come to the street outside the garden. But she continued to lock the garden at dusk.

The apparitions continued, and a large crowd awaited the children each evening. The crowd grew constantly, and people came even from the Flemish-speaking section of the country.

Beginning on December 6 or 7 the children were taken to the convent after each apparition and were questioned separately by doctors and others. Extensive notes were taken during these questionings, and these notes constitute an invaluable document.

On several occasions Our Lady told the children that she wished them to be present on the Feast of the Immaculate Conception. Because that date had been specifically mentioned, the crowd was even larger than usual on December 8. About 15,000 people were there. Many people were expecting a great miracle on that day. Something interesting did happen, but it was nothing that could be seen by the great majority of people in the crowd.

The children arrived at ten minutes after six. They were escorted by their parents and accompanied by four doctors. The children beheld the vision as soon as they took their customary places in the street. Our Lady was more beautiful than ever.

Dr. Maistriaux felt Albert's pulse. Albert turned to look at the doctor and then turned back to the vision.

Little Gilberte wept. Dr. Maistriaux asked her why.

"Because she is so beautiful," Gilberte answered.

A few moments later Dr. Maistriaux asked Gilberte the same question but received no answer. The girl had not heard him. Then the doctor again took Albert's pulse. The boy's eyes did not leave the vision; he did not even know the doctor was there.

Dr. Lurquin of Houyet held a lighted match under Big Gilberte's left hand and held it there until the fire had consumed half the match. She did not notice it. Other doctors pinched, slapped, and pricked the five children. They shined flashlights into their eyes. There was no reaction.

When the vision was over, Fernande said: "I could see nothing, neither fence, nor tree, nor crowd; only the Holy Virgin who smiled at us."

The doctors examined Gilberte Voisin's hand and could not find any trace of burning.

"Just think of that, Daddy," she said. "They tried to make me believe that they had pricked and burned me."

The first phase of the apparitions ended on December 8. Until this time the Virgin had appeared suddenly to the children with little waiting. After December 8 the children had to wait for her, and on some evenings she did not come at all. The children said the Rosary while they waited and then crashed to their knees the instant she appeared.

On December 17, Our Lady asked for "a chapel."

Four days later she said: "I am the Immaculate Virgin."

On December 23, Fernande asked: "Why do you come?"

Our Lady answered: "That people might come here on pilgrimages."

On December 28 she said: "Soon I shall appear for the last time."

On December 29 the Blessed Virgin opened her arms in the usual gesture of farewell, and when she did so Fernande saw in the region of the Virgin's chest a heart of gold surrounded by glittering rays. The other four children did not see the heart on this occasion. The next day three of the children saw the heart of gold. In addition to Fernande it was seen by Big Gilberte and by Andree.

On this occasion Our Lady said to Fernande:

"Pray. Pray very much."

On the last day of the year, December 31, 1932, all five children saw Mary's heart of gold. The heart would be seen in all the remaining apparitions.

This heart, one of the most distinctive features of the Beauraing apparitions, was, of course, the Immaculate Heart of Mary. This establishes an obvious link with Fatima, where the Immaculate Heart was also an important feature. More will be said about this later.

On December 30, in addition to showing her heart to three of the children, Our Lady said:

"Pray. Pray very much."

On January 1 she said to Gilberte Voisin:

"Pray always."

On January 2, she said:

"Tomorrow I will speak to each one of you separately."

A great crowd was on hand for what was to be the final appearance, January 3, 1933. After two decades of the Rosary four of the children gave a joyful shout and fell to their knees. Fernande sobbed because she could not see the vision.

The Virgin was even more resplendent than usual when she appeared to the four children. She also smiled more than usual.

She spoke first to Little Gilberte. Leaning forward, she said to the girl: "This is between you and me, and I ask you to speak of it to no one." Then she told Gilberte a secret that has never been revealed. After that she said: "Good-by."

Gilberte wept, because she knew that never again in this life would she see the Blessed Virgin.

Next Our Lady spoke to Big Gilberte. To her, she uttered the words that are considered the Great Promise of Beauraing:

"I will convert sinners."

After that she told Big Gilberte a secret and said: "Good-by."

She told Albert a secret and said: "Good-by."

To Andree she said:

"I am the Mother of God, the Queen of Heaven. Pray always."

Then she said "good-by" to Andree while disappearing from the four children. She showed the heart of gold as she disappeared.

When the vision was over, Fernande, who was grief stricken at not seeing the Virgin, remained kneeling after the other children had gone into the convent to be questioned. Suddenly she heard a loud noise like a clap of thunder and saw a ball of fire on the hawthorn. Many other people also heard this noise and saw the fire. Then Fernande saw the Blessed Virgin.

Because Our Lady had saved Fernande's message till last and because of the dramatic way in which it was presented, it seems likely that she wished to place special emphasis on these words.

"Do you love my Son?" Our Lady asked.

"Yes."

"Do you love me?"

"Yes."

"Then sacrifice yourself for me."

Fernande wished to ask questions. What kinds of sacrifices should she make? Should she enter the religious life?

But the Virgin did not give her a chance to ask the questions. She glowed more brilliantly than before and extended her arms in the gesture of farewell. As she did so, she showed the heart of gold. As she disappeared, she said: "Good-by."

Fernande, knowing that this was the last vision of the beautiful Virgin, wept and sank to the ground. Strong arms bore her up and helped her into the convent.

During the early stages of the apparitions the people of Beauraing had greeted the story with great skepticism. It seemed impossible that the Blessed Virgin should appear in their village and to five such "ordinary" children. Some villagers said that the children were sincere but deluded. Others said they were frauds who enjoyed the attention they were receiving. The parents, who did not believe the story at first, suffered greatly because they were the laughingstock of the town.

Mr. and Mrs. Voisin were among the first to believe in the apparitions. As time went on, and as more and more of the villagers saw the children during the apparition, the skepticism all but disappeared. It was evident that the children really were seeing something. Mrs. Degeimbre became convinced about the time of the last apparition. Mother Theophile and

Father Lambert came to believe very firmly in the apparitions. Even hardened Socialists were convinced, and some of them returned to the Church. The story of the apparitions caused a great sensation all over Europe. In 1933 and 1934 it was fashionable to "expose" Beauraing, and many books and magazine articles were written for this purpose. Some of these attacks were made by enemies of religion who did not believe in any kind of supernatural manifestation. Others were written by sincere Catholics who thought that the five children had been deluded or were frauds. Despite the surface furor, the ordinary Belgian Catholics were inclined from the start to believe in the apparitions. Two million pilgrims visited the hawthorn in the year 1933. In the end it was the common people and not the critics who proved to be correct. Gradually doubt and skepticism disappeared as the facts of the story became known and as the results were observed.

The children remained in Beauraing for some time and led lives as close to normal as was possible under the circumstances. They visited the hawthorn tree each day to say the Rosary. They never benefited financially from the apparitions; in fact the families suffered financial losses. The crowds of pilgrims and curiosity seekers trampled down the gardens that belonged to the Degeimbres, and they forced the closing of the little shop which had been run by Mrs. Voisin. Both families bore such ordeals with amazing patience.

From the very beginning there were reports of amazing physical cures that had taken place at the shrine. Some of these reports were impossible to refute and helped quell the attacks on Beauraing.

There was, for example, the case of Maria Van Laer of Turnhout, in northern Belgium. Miss Van Laer, a patient in a hospital conducted by the Franciscan Sisters of the Holy Family, had been a helpless invalid for sixteen of her thirty-three years. Hers was a tubercular condition. Her spinal column was deformed, one of her legs was diseased, and she had large tumors which had developed into open sores. The doctors said that an operation would be fatal, and they held no hope for her recovery.

Miss Van Laer was taken to Beauraing on June 23, 1933. This, it will be noted, was less than six months after the last apparition. Miss Van Laer's stretcher was taken to the hawthorn, and she remained there for some time. Then she asked to see one of the five children. She was taken to the Degeimbre home where she talked with Gilberte and Mrs. Degeimbre. Then she went back to the hawthorn. During the second visit she found herself able to move for the first time in years. She slept in the ambulance on the way home. When she reached Turnhout shortly after midnight she awoke and found herself cured. No pains, no tumors, no sores, and no deformities! Today Miss Van Laer is Sister Pudentia of the Franciscan Sisters of the Holy Family and leads an active life as portress at the convent and as a visiting nurse. As we shall see later, her cure has been declared a miracle.

"I will convert sinners," Our Lady said to the five children, and she has carried out her promise. Among the earliest of the converts were Mr. and Mrs. Hector Voisin. Mrs. Voisin returned to the Sacraments while the apparitions were still going on, and even before Our Lady made her Great Promise. Mr. Voisin returned at Easter, 1933. We can imagine the happiness of Gilberte Voisin when she saw her parents attending Mass and receiving Communion. Her prayers had been answered.

Among the most famous of the converts was a young man who had given up his faith and who had become a Communist. He was made editor of the Belgian Communist newspaper *Le Drapeau Rouge* (*The Red Flag*). During the German occupation of Belgium, in World War II, he was arrested by the Germans and his life was in great danger. While he was in prison he remembered the Blessed Virgin, and he promised her that he would return to the faith if he should be freed. He was released, but he failed to keep his promise. He was imprisoned again and freed again. Still he did not return to the faith.

In September 1945 the young man was struck by the thought that he should visit Beauraing. He did not know where the thought came from, and he tried to banish it. But the thought would not go away; it haunted him. Almost against his will he found himself at Beauraing although he did not have the least faith. He stood facing the hawthorn. Suddenly he was thrown to the ground. "I was trying to protect myself from the fall," he said, "and I fell, hanging onto the back of the last bench. For a long time I saw nothing but the figure of Our Lady in the hawthorn. A complete transformation was produced in me. I cried over my past life. But I also cried for joy, conscious that something new had entered my soul."

The next day the former Communist editor went to confession and received Holy Communion. He now receives Communion every day. He is a fervent tertiary of St. Dominic. It was through him that the Legion of Mary was established in Belgium.

Many other conversions have been reported among people from many different countries. These conversions are called Beauraing's Great Invisible Treasure.

In 1935 the Bishop of Namur, the diocese in which Beauraing is located, appointed an episcopal commission to investigate the events. The Bishop died, and the investigation continued under his successor, Bishop Andre-Marie Charue. On February 2, 1943, the Bishop authorized public devotions to "Our Lady of Beauraing." Then on July 2, 1949, the Bishop released two important documents relating to Beauraing. One was an episcopal decree declaring that two of the many cures credited to Our Lady of Beauraing were authentic miracles. One of the cures was that of Maria Van Laer. The other was the cure of Mrs. Acar, who had been cured of a tumor of the womb on July 30, 1933.

The other document of July 2, 1949, was a letter from the Bishop to the clergy of his diocese. The Bishop said: "We are able in all serenity and prudence to affirm that the Queen of Heaven appeared to the children of Beauraing during the winter of 1932–33 especially to show us in her maternal Heart the anxious appeal for prayer and the promise of her powerful mediation for the conversion of sinners."

Pious Catholics of Belgium were delighted. They had been sure all along that the Blessed Virgin had appeared to the five children of Beauraing. Now they had official recognition of the fact.

The shrine began to develop after the Bishop recognized the cult in 1943. The Bishop blessed a large statue of Our Lady of Beauraing on August 22, 1946, the Feast of the Immaculate Heart. The statue stands under the hawthorn where Our Lady appeared. The cornerstone of the chapel requested by Our Lady was laid on the Feast of the Immaculate Heart, 1947, and the chapel was consecrated August 21, 1954. The chapel with its many confessionals gives Our Lady the opportunity to convert sinners. The hawthorn tree was surrounded by bronze railings which serve as a gigantic votive candle stand. An open-air altar stands on the spot formerly occupied by the Lourdes grotto. The former convent and Academy have been converted into a home for sick pilgrims.

An old feudal castle and its surrounding grounds have been purchased and are used as a sort of annex to the shrine. Ceremonies are held there on days when the former convent garden will not accommodate the crowds. The castle is being used as a retreat house, and a beautiful basilica will be built on the grounds.

The story of Beauraing spread rapidly throughout Europe, and many pilgrimages went to the shrine. At present the shrine is visited by about one million pilgrims a year.

Slowly, the story is also becoming known throughout the rest of the free world. The first official pilgrimage from the United States arrived at Beauraing in September 1953.

What has happened to the five children of Beauraing? All five have married and now have children of their own.

Andree Degeimbre has never left Beauraing. Her husband is a nurseryman who, because of ill health, is not able to work full time at his trade. To supplement the family income, Andree maintains a religious-goods shop in the front of their house. They have three children. Andree leads the Rosary at the hawthorn every night at 6:30, summer or winter.

Gilberte Voisin moved back to Beauraing after her husband, a state policeman, was killed in an accident in 1953. She has two children.

Gilberte Degeimbre lives in Brussels and has two children. Fernande Voisin lives in Namur and has five children. Albert has three children. He is training native teachers in the Belgian Congo.

All five have great devotion to the Blessed Mother, and they are bringing up their children to have devotion to her also. All five shun the limelight. They are not important, they say. They were merely the instruments through whom Our Lady gave her message to the world. It is the Blessed Virgin who is important at Beauraing.

Some people have expressed surprise that the children married instead of entering the religious life, but the children merely followed the vocations which they believed God had sent them.

"According to our way of looking at sanctity," said one prelate, "these children should have entered a convent at a very early age and died of consumption at the age of twenty-two. The Blessed Virgin probably has a different way of looking at things."

To this, Dom Hughes Delogne, O.S.B., adds: "In fact, the Blessed Virgin was married. She obtained the first miracle from her Son at a wedding, and she obtained it for married people. Christ Himself raised marriage to the dignity of a sacrament. Maybe the Mother of God judged that in our era . . . it was supremely important to give the example of real Christian homes."

Some people have complained that while the Blessed Mother appeared thirty-three times at Beauraing she said very little. Actually, the words which she spoke are very important, and her message consists of more than spoken words. She did not mention her Immaculate Heart, for example, but she showed it as a Heart of Gold, and this action was more eloquent than words.

The most obvious comment to make about the Message of Beauraing is that it is a repetition and a reemphasis of the Message of Fatima. Let's examine this feature first. Then we shall examine the features which make the Message of Beauraing distinctive.

If Our Lady's words at Fatima can be summed up briefly, we find that she had three principal requests: (1) prayer, especially the Rosary; (2) sacrifice; (3) devotion to her Immaculate Heart. All these things are included in the Message of Beauraing: "Pray. Pray very much." "Pray always." The Rosary was not featured as prominently at Beauraing as at Fatima, but it was there. During her latter visions Our Lady wore a rosary on her arm, and she appeared while the children were saying the Rosary. She asked for sacrifice: "Sacrifice yourself for me." And she featured her Heart to such an extent that Our Lady of Beauraing is often called the Virgin with the Golden Heart. The Feast of the Immaculate Heart of Mary, August 22, is also the official Beauraing feast. In all these things Our Lady of Beauraing seems to be saying: "I gave you a very important Message at Fatima. I am repeating that Message now. Please act upon it."

But Our Lady of Beauraing does not stop there. She goes on to stress some of her most important titles and prerogatives. "The Marian tenor of the Message is very remarkable," said Dom Cyrille Lambot, O.S.B., in a report to the International Marian Congress in Rome in 1954. "The great aspects of the Mystery of Mary—her person and her mission—are assembled. . . ."

"I am the Immaculate Virgin," Mary said at Beauraing. At Lourdes she had said, "I am the Immaculate Conception," which means that she was conceived without original sin. The statement at Beauraing is even more sweeping and reminds us of her sinless life and the fact that she never committed even the smallest venial sin. The statement also reminds us of her Virginity which she consecrated to God.

"I am the Mother of God." Here Mary called herself by her most important title. All her other titles, all her prerogatives, stem from the fact that she is the Mother of God.

"I am . . . the Queen of Heaven." The idea of her Queenship was also emphasized by the rays that surrounded her head during the Beauraing apparitions. Here, Mary reminds us of the great power that is hers. She reigns in heaven with her Son, who is King.

The doctrine of Mary's Queenship has been receiving great attention in modern times. In 1949, Pope Pius XII said: "Jesus is King throughout all eternity by nature and by right of conquest; through Him, with Him, and subordinate to Him, Mary is Queen by grace, by divine relationship, by right of conquest, and by singular election. And her kingdom is as vast as that of her Son and God, since nothing is excluded from her domain."

In 1954, Pope Pius XII established a new feast for the Universal Church, the Feast of the Queenship of Mary. This is celebrated every year on May 31.

"I will convert sinners." This is the Great Promise of Beauraing and probably its most distinctive feature. Mary has mentioned sin in almost all apparitions of the past hundred and fifty years. She has wept over the sins of the world (La Salette), and she has threatened the world with punishment for its sins (Fatima). At Beauraing she did not weep and she did not threaten. She made the simple but breath-taking promise: "I will convert sinners." There were no conditions to this, although we know, of course, that she will be able to convert more sinners if she has our prayers and sacrifices.

How can Mary, a creature, say, "I will convert sinners"? Should not she have said, "I will obtain the conversion of sinners"? The only answer seems to be that God has entrusted tremendous power to Mary and that He refuses her nothing. She is the Mediatrix of All Graces in the full sense of the term. All our prayers and requests go to God through Mary, and she distributes all the graces that come from God. Mary's Universal Mediation is not yet a dogma of the Church, but most theologians accept the idea. It is interesting to note that Belgium was the first country in the world to have an indult to celebrate a special feast in honor of Mary's Mediation.

"Do you love my Son? Do you love Me? Then sacrifice yourself for me."

These words emphasize the union of Jesus and Mary. To love one is to love the other; the love of Mary brings us inevitably to the love of Christ. The last sentence, with which Our Lady ended the Message of Beauraing, shows the importance of penance and reparation, both of which are included in the idea of sacrifice.

At Beauraing we see Mary as the Immaculate Virgin, the Mother of God, the Queen of Heaven, the Mediatrix who will convert sinners. Dom Cyrille Lambot, O.S.B., who was quoted earlier, adds: "But at Beauraing these privileges and prerogatives appear under their glorious aspect, especially when the Virgin, already resplendent, shows her shining heart as pure gold. She is the triumphant Virgin in the war against Satan and sin."

The whole message is a most consoling one for each one of us. We have a powerful friend in heaven—the Queen herself. And she loves us with the same Immaculate Heart that was fashioned to give a Mother's love to the God-Man. God can refuse Mary nothing. As long as we stay close to her, we have nothing to fear.

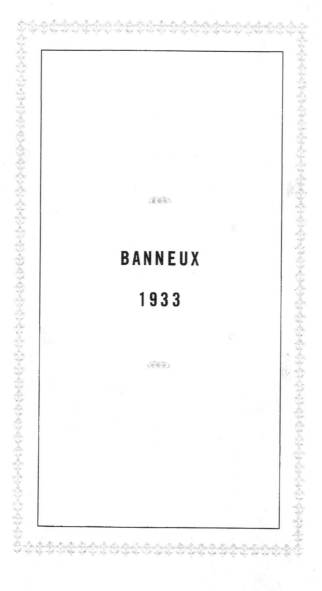

BANNEUX

1933

THE VIRGIN
OF THE POOR

Robert M. Maloy, S.M.

When, twelve days after the last apparition at
Beauraing, news first began to circulate of
miraculous happenings fifty miles to the
north in the Belgian hamlet of Banneux, the
suspicion of sound people was alerted. One
of the earliest chroniclers of Banneux,
Armand Geradin, at first only laughed and
with humor suggested, "Beauraing, second
edition." Those familiar with the history of
Lourdes subsequent to Bernadette Soubirous
were alarmed lest the impostor, the neurotic,
and even the diabolically possessed should
here besmirch true religious devotion to the
great delight of the Marxian Socialists and
anti-clericals of Belgium.

None was more cautious than the devoted
chaplain of Banneux, Abbé Louis Jamin, a
young priest of twenty-nine years, who,

although he had a Sodality of Our Lady in his parish and a Marian devotion of sorts, still paid little attention to the facts of Lourdes and regarded pilgrimages as largely the workings of superstition. When he first heard on that wintry Monday afternoon that his struggling parish had been singled out for a heavenly apparition the prior evening, a good-natured smile accompanied his observation: "We don't see the Blessed Virgin as easily as that. Mariette has heard talk of the children of Beauraing, and she thinks she has seen the Blessed Virgin!" But Father Jamin soon had to change his skeptical mind for that of the humble observer and verifier of the fact that the supernatural not only surpasses the prosaic patterns designed by reason, but has a total logic of its own, granting nothing but complete acceptance.

Father Jamin's immediate firsthand knowledge of Mariette Beco, the visionary of Banneux, went back some five years to February 1928, when for reasons of health the Bishop of Liége had assigned him to the leisure of a small parish in the village of Banneux. The three hundred souls confided to his care on the marshy plateau ten miles from Liége resembled spiritually the barren landscape and the dull flatness of the plain. The great pall of religious indifference and boredom enveloping the laboring class had descended here as elsewhere in Belgium and throughout Europe. Comfortable bourgeois religious values with which the Church had become identified were unreal and incapable of dealing with the daily hunger and thirst man has for genuine justice, love, and worship. Well could a pontiff call the great scandal of the day the loss of the working classes to the Church. It was with such a background that Mariette Beco, the twelve-year-old girl, who had been born on March 25, the Feast of the Annunciation, 1921, and who was privileged to be the instrument through which the message of Banneux comes to us, was familiar.

The young curé had observed that Mariette was the sturdy, outdoor type, animated by a practical peasant spirit with a strongheadedness which repeatedly through the years earned her the reputation of being *farouche*, anti-social. Father Jamin's cursory evaluation of Mariette's physical state was supported by the village physician, Dr. Heuse, who examined Mariette and found her a healthy and robust child—normal in all ways.

The Beco family lived in that stretch of the northern Ardennes where Belgium reaches toward the Dutch and German borders. To arrive at their humble dwelling in Banneux, it is necessary to travel uphill, regardless of your approach to the somewhat rarefied atmosphere of the plateau hamlet.

To locate Banneux immediately, it is necessary first to find Liége, venerable capital of the east Belgian province of the same name, whose political and ecclesiastical organization dates from at least 980. Banneux is some ten miles to the southeast of Liége. A favorite route of the Banneux pilgrims of the Blessed Virgin is the Liége-Verviers train with its short whistle stop at Fraipont, directly east of Liége and to the north of the shrine. From Fraipont many follow the winding back roads up through the woods to the Virgin, reciting their rosaries and stopping to meditate at the fifteen rosary stations along the way.

Those not mounting to Banneux-Notre-Dame along the northern valley of the Vesdre River might be coming up from Spa, the renowned health resort to the southeast, through the rustic Hoegne Valley with its rushing streams. The motorist from the west can travel the national Liége-Louveigné-Pepinster highway through the Ourthe Valley till it gently climbs to Banneux. The southern pilgrim from the direction of Luxembourg would want to approach the shrine through the Amblève Valley, famous for its caverns at Remouchamps.

The Beco home could easily have been passed by unnoticed during the long winter evenings, for little light or sign of life would be seen from the ribbon of road which is the Louveigné-Pepinster artery as it enters a pine woods a few yards from the four-room house built by Julien Beco for his wife and family, which was soon to grow to eleven.

Such would have been the case January 15, 1933, when by seven o'clock all had retired except Mrs. Beco, who was busy caring for the youngest child, Marie-Louise, and Mariette, who was waiting up for her brother Julien, who had been missing since noon. Mariette, as the eldest, was an immense aid to her mother as a practical little housekeeper and one who could be given the responsibility of the younger children. At the moment her attention was torn between keeping supper warm for Julien, the ten-year-old vagabond, glancing out the window in search of him, and watching over her young brother, René, asleep in his crib. In the Fagne—Banneux's marshes—work was long and hard, as farming the muddy soil, which has the appearance of unproductive desolation, was a strenuous occupation. The father, Julien Beco, had simple tastes— no paper, no tavern—and his great pleasure seems to have been the deep peace of sleep after the exhaustion of the daily toil necessary to support his large family.

The evening of January 15 was no exception to his usual regimen as he fell soundly asleep, still fully dressed, in the rear room of the cramped, angular house. Two of the Beco boys, Alphonse and André, were asleep upstairs and Simon was with his father. The front room of the ground floor was a multi-purpose family room, whose rhythm was dictated by the preparation of frugal meals on the simple stove. Here Mariette and her mother were still occupied.

Impatient and fretting over Julien's return, Mariette again knelt on the little bench under the large, single front window and lifted the bed sheet which doubled as a curtain. This time suddenly Mariette noticed a light in the small yard in front of the house; against the total darkness of the winter night she made out a lovely lady, seeming to be all light. The lady was young, beautiful, and had a most gracious smile. As Mariette looked out the window, the vision was to her right. The youth, radiant beauty, and gracious motherly smile of the visitor who bent her head and shoulders slightly to the left while looking toward Mariette so grasped the child that at first only a gasp of awesome wonder and surprise escaped in a staccato, "Ah."

Quickly, however, Mariette's spirited practicality took over as she minutely examined the lady, noting the great oval light which enveloped her body; the gown, which was spotless and dazzlingly white, chastely closed at the collar and falling in the simple dignity of broad pleats; the sash, an unforgettable sky blue, loosely fashioned around the waist and terminating in two streamers at the vision's left knee. Covering the lady's head, shoulders, and arms was a veil as completely white as her gown, but of a transparent material. The lady was inclined to the left and forward, with the hem of her dress slightly lifted, exposing her right foot crowned with a golden rose. On her right arm hung a rosary of diamond-like brilliancy, whose golden chain and cross reflected in the light.

The lady's hands, folded together as is usual in prayer, imparted an air of familiarity as their fingers pointed downward, not upward. This was Our Lady's first meeting with Mariette and was intensely personal. Later apparitions which brought the formal message of Banneux, while losing nothing of their gracious dignity and intimacy, showed the hands pointed heavenward as in formal prayer.

Rubbing her eyes to make sure this was no trick of sight, Mariette decided the oil lamp was causing a hallucination. Here was the explanation. Move the light, remove the vision. This done, the luminous young woman still remained, regarding Mariette with eyes and smile of infinite kindness. If her little methods of science would not dispel the lightsome lady, Mariette could be afraid. "Mama, there's a woman in the garden!" "Nonsense!" Mrs. Beco echoed with a preoccupied shrug of the shoulders. In a stammered contradiction Mariette added, "A lovely lady, beautifully dressed: a completely white dress, a blue sash." Amused, Mrs. Beco suggested, "Oh yes! Perhaps it is the Blessed Virgin." But to silence the foolishness, the mother looked out the window and then, somewhat fearfully, perceived a white light in the general form of a person of normal size, slightly bent to the left, and wearing what appeared to be a sheet over its head. She could not make out the distinct features that Mariette was seeing. With alarm she declared, "It is a witch!" and brusquely closed the sheet over the window.

Mariette, now certain that she saw something, opened the sheet and positively reiterated, in her strongheaded way, "No, it is really the Blessed Virgin. She smiles at me; she is so beautiful." Reassured by the youthful visitor, Mariette's fear completely vanished, and she started to pray on the rosary she had found by chance on the old road to neighboring Tancremont. After several decades in which Mariette saw the Lady's lips also moving in prayer, a startling innovation in the history of all Marian apparitions took place. The Lady, placing her left hand on her breast, lifted her right to the level of her head and beckoned Mariette with her index finger. As Mariette made for the front door, which was to the right of the window and opened close to the spot where the vision stood, her mother firmly intercepted her and locked the door. Mariette hastened back to the window, but the visitor had already departed; she knelt and prayed the Rosary for about ten minutes.

When the vagabond Julien returned, in typical brother fashion he shuffled off as girlish foolishness his sister's allusion to having seen "something beautiful." The father similarly dismissed the next morning's announcement of Mariette's vision with a brusque, "You're a fool." However, later when Mrs. Beco also remarked on the Sunday evening happenings, his curiosity was piqued, and he had his wife and daughter separately indicate the spot of the apparition.

Absent from all religious influence for years and the victim of the skepticism which ruled even the popular Belgian mind, he evolved a theory of light reflection to explain away the supernatural happening and experimented with the oil lamp and the reflection of its light from the frozen ice. It proved nothing more than Mariette's similar experiment and aroused his interest and sympathy.

With self-control remarkable for a twelve-year-old girl, Mariette made no mention of the appearance of the Lady except to her friend Josephine Leonard, whom she told privately under the chestnut tree in the school yard during Monday morning's ten o'clock recess. Josephine took up the challenge of the supposed joke and teased Mariette until she broke into tears. That the school tomboy, who just last week had won a decisive victory over several boys, would succumb to the weakness of tears instinctively convinced the Leonard girl that this was something for the pastor, Father Jamin.

Using the necessity of returning a book to the parish library as an excuse, the two girls rang the bell of the rectory at four o'clock Monday afternoon, and Josephine as the *diplomate extraordinaire* acquainted the pastor with the facts. At his first skeptical reaction, Mariette bolted from the house with some of the speed which had helped her win more than one athletic contest in the school yard. An indignant stomp of the foot accented Mariette's, "I know well what I've seen; I am sure of it."

On Monday there was no repetition of the apparition. Tuesday morning for the first time since the previous October 29, Mariette was at Mass, and to the astonishment of the priest she showed up for catechism class. If she were to see the Blessed Virgin again, Mariette figured, she must be worthy. But Tuesday also passed without any special happenings.

When Wednesday morning's catechism lesson came off perfectly, causing Father Jamin to record the first mark which he could remember that hadn't been a zero, the priest began to suspect a possible link between the blurted report of Josephine on Monday and the unexpected change in Mariette. To the gentle proddings of the priest in an informal, after-class session, Mariette responded with a simplicity and directness which convinced him of her sincerity, but not of her freedom from illusion. During this first interview session, carefully and immediately recorded, Father Jamin repeatedly tried to trip Mariette by attempting to identify the vision with a statue of Our Lady of Lourdes in the parish church. Mariette firmly maintained the Lady in the garden was bent forward and to the left; the statue in the church was different, and not nearly so beautiful.

Despite her natural fear of the darkness of the night-shrouded Fagne, Mariette suddenly left the house at seven o'clock, Wednesday evening, January 18. Her father followed and saw her kneel and say her Rosary on the edge of the walk which led from the three steps of the house to the fence at the edge of the road. His attempts to arouse her from the bitter cold and darkness of the night met with no response. He could not, for some unusual reason, bring himself to touch her. Suddenly he noticed that the child lifted her arms. Visible only to Mariette, the Virgin, all-luminous, reappeared, descending from between the tops of two tall pines.

Gradually she became larger and soon was standing but five feet away from the child, resting on a smokish gray cloud about a foot from the earth. Mariette observed that the vision's head was surrounded by rays of light, which resembled long and short "pencils." (Here, of course, is a great similarity to Beauraing.) With her hands piously folded, the lady moved her lips as though she were joining in Mariette's Rosary, but she did not touch the white rosary which hung over her right forearm.

Meanwhile, the distraught father walked to the rear of the house, then returned and re-entered the front door, slamming it and turning the key noisily. He immediately came out again and shouted, "Without a doubt you're going crazy!" Despite this display of annoyance, he still instinctively feared to touch her.

When he realized how out of the ordinary Mariette's actions were, Julien got out his bicycle and headed toward the rectory. But as luck would have it, Father Jamin was not back from his weekly trip to Liège. Beco's next effort was to alert his cousin Michael Charlesèche, and the two men, with Charlesèche's eleven-year-old son, returned on foot. During all this time Mariette had remained praying before the pleasantly smiling eyes and lips of the Lady, who was still bowed in that charming symbol of motherly attention to Mariette. She repeated her gesture of Sunday's apparition, beckoning with her finger, but this time Mariette was free to obey. The Lady, floating on the cloud, glided through the opening in the fence into the road and drew Mariette after her. "Where are you going? Come back!" her father cried frantically. Without turning or stopping, Mariette gave the only possible answer, "She calls me!"

Three times Mariette's progress on the road was interrupted, as she dropped with a thud to her knees on the frozen earth each time the Lady stopped.

Suddenly Beco, Charlesèche, and the boy, who were following at a distance of some twenty-five yards, saw the child sharply turn right from the road and fall to her knees on the side of a ditch before a previously unknown spring. The Lady directed Mariette, "Place your hands in the water," and without the least hesitation Mariette followed the instructions, and the splash of Mariette's hand in the stream could be heard. Then, speaking aloud so that the witnesses easily heard, Mariette said, "This stream is reserved for me," and "Good evening. *Au revoir.*" The vision ended as suddenly as it began, and the Lady became smaller as she disappeared above the pines alongside the ditch.

The three witnesses crowded about Mariette who seemed to awake from a trancelike state and notice them for the first time. Their questioning brought out the fact that Mariette's words were but repetitions of the Lady's during the thirty-five-minute visit.

By eight-thirty, Father Jamin had been informed of the happenings. Taking with him a Benedictine priest living close to Banneux, Father Boniface del Marmol, he arrived at the Becos' near ten o'clock to find Mariette soundly asleep. But already the important work of Banneux was beginning. As the priest was leaving, Mariette's father approached

Father Jamin and requested to see him the next day to confess and receive Communion! On the way to the Beco home Father Jamin had mentioned to the Benedictine that he wished heaven would give him some sign, "for example, if Mariette's father were converted"!

Though Mariette kept the happenings entirely to herself, with the exception of Josephine Leonard, who was such a silent confidante that neither Josephine's mother nor her sister were to learn of the apparitions for still another week, Father Jamin continued to gather information and kept his bishop informed. But in the future he kept away from the Beco house and the scene of the spring and received further reports through the intermediary of sound and trusted witnesses.

At seven o'clock the following evening, Thursday, January 19, Mariette hurriedly threw an old overcoat over her head and, walking but a few paces from the front stairs, knelt down in the snow and started to pray in a low voice. Hardly had two decades been recited when the child stretched out her arms with the excited announcement, "Oh, she is here!" Mariette then asked a question: "Who are you, lovely Lady?" The immediate response of the Lady was something so entirely new that for many it constitutes the special appeal of Banneux—"I am the Virgin of the Poor."

With several silent observers following, Mariette and the vision, apparent to her alone, made their way to the spring, repeating the sudden halts and genuflections of the previous evening on the road. Kneeling at the source, Mariette posed her second question, "Beautiful Lady, yesterday you said, 'This spring is reserved for me.' Why for me?" Our Lady seemed amused at Mariette's personal application of her words and quickly impressed the universal character of Banneux by declaring: "This spring is reserved for all nations—to relieve the sick." Although Mariette later asked the meaning of "na-ti-on" and only understood when a map of the world was produced, and was not exactly sure of the sense of the French word "relieve" (*soulager*), she was instinctively grateful for the words of this ever-smiling Lady: "Thank you, thank you." Now as a most delicate echo Mariette repeated in a distinct voice the Virgin's words, "I shall pray for you. *Au revoir.*" And the entire apparition ended, having taken approximately seven minutes.

The tension of the great joy of seeing Our Lady during the previous four days and the anger and impatience when she was disbelieved kept an exhausted Mariette in bed all day Friday, January 20. She arose around six forty-five in the evening and announced her intentions of keeping her wintry appointment with Our Lady. It was no wonder her parents expressed concern over her fatigue and opposed her intentions. The Becos, despite their basic acceptance of Christian teaching by raising a large family in their poor circumstances, had failed to temper the natural wildness of their offspring by Christian training in respect, obedience, and consideration. At the Becos' there was no trace of formality or ceremony. Thus Mariette's none too delicate insistence that she would jump from the window if her parents didn't permit her to go out, carried the day, especially since thirty people had gathered in the yard.

Her father, who had been present and evinced a growing belief in the truth of the supernatural happenings ever since the second apparition, appeared at the front door with Mariette and accompanied her the several feet to her position on the gravel walk. After several minutes of Hail Marys recited in a demi-voice, Mariette opened her arms and exclaimed with naturalness and simplicity, "Here she is!" The child then shortly inquired in a voice clearly audible to the bystanders, "What do you wish, my beautiful Lady?" The Virgin of the Poor appeared as usual tonight, but this evening she had a request to make—"I would like a small chapel." The witnesses had this relayed by Mariette who said, "Oh, a small chapel," just before she leaned slightly forward and crumpled to the ground unconscious. When one of the two physicians in attendance, Dr. Chaumont, examined the child, he found her pulse normal and discovered nothing to become upset about. Mariette recovered consciousness within two or three minutes and then submitted to the interrogations of the visitors.

Of special interest was the ending of this vision, which lasted only two to three minutes. The Virgin just before departing unfolded her hands from their prayerful position, imposed them on Mariette, and then with her right hand, blessed Mariette with the sign of the cross. It was at this point that the collapse came. While she gave these details to her interrogators, Mariette was on the bed where she had been placed. At the doctor's suggestion as soon as she completed her description of the essential points, the visionary was permitted to fall into a deep peaceful sleep.

When Mariette reported for her interview with Father Jamin on Saturday afternoon at two forty-five, he gently went over the facts of the case. As a priest, Father Jamin realized that whether or not he liked the role, he was the foremost official representative of the Church in Banneux and that he must scrupulously gather objective data regarding these possibly supernatural happenings which might affect the life of his parish. Thus after every apparition Mariette had to report to him. He did not believe in the apparitions and systematically held that this was a case of illusion. His smiles revealed his feelings before which Mariette could offer through her tears only the persistent and defiant protest: "I saw her; I heard her!" Father Jamin suggested, probably half hoping to end the affair, that the unique blessing of the fourth appearance was a sign of the end of the apparitions.

Despite the family flare-up of the previous evening, the Becos presented no opposition to Mariette's attempts to keep her usual rendezvous with Our Lady. She took her position in the yard and began her wait for the Virgin. After some time one of the usual witnesses asked if she saw anything. Rising, Mariette declared she saw nothing: "It is finished; the Virgin blessed me yesterday; she will not come any more." Despite Mariette's strong conviction that the visions were over, each evening she prayed two or three Rosaries and sometimes as many as six or seven. The curiosity seekers soon fell off until some evenings Mariette alone kept the vigil near the snowy pines. Other nights only her father would join her.

With but her father's old overcoat thrown over her head and shoulders, she knelt on a sack on the narrow path, constantly watching the opening between the pines where Our Lady usually first appeared. Each night for three weeks the vigil was kept, and after each fruitless watch Mariette's conviction grew that the Lady would never return. With a pang of disappointment, she repeated each night, "She did not come this evening."

What a difference there is between Lourdes and Banneux. Where Bernadette Soubirous only infrequently bore the taunts of the world's cruelest tormentors, school children, Mariette's daily attendance at catechism class and school was a continuous trial. The boys would genuflect before Mariette asking her blessing, and one day they beat her up so badly that she carried black and blue marks on her face for some time. The girls would give vulgar imitations of Our Lady and then with great glee sing out, "Good morning, Bernadette." One night, as she prayed alone in the yard, some local rogues attempted to frighten her. Her grandmother and aunts ridiculed her. Where Bernadette was of the very poor, Mariette was of the poorest of the poor, for not only were material assets lacking, but her family and neighbors had severed themselves from the roots of Christian tradition, whereas the Soubirouses were deeply religious people. The very day of the first Banneux apparition marked another Sunday on which Mariette had missed Mass. Her family indifferently ignored the supernatural, and when Mariette became discouraged over catechism in October of 1932 her father told her not to go back to the church if it was so difficult and embarrassing. She took him up on this suggestion.

Actually, once the apparitions became common knowledge, Mariette's father bore the lash of the local Socialists, who amused themselves in ridiculing the now converted Julien as a pillar of the Church.

Still, the only thing that brought tears to Mariette's eyes was the accusation of some witnesses that "She is putting on a pious show," when everything seemed to indicate the contrary. If a child of twelve, who showed up poorly on the Binet-Simon tests, had been able to manage such a complex and imaginative piece of dramatic art, consistent not only in details, but also succinct and theologically sound, why did she not turn aside derision and continue the jest during the long weeks of fruitless vigil? Psychological disturbance had been considered and dropped after detailed medical consideration could trace no natural cause for the phenomenon either before, during, or after the apparitions. The child was simply normal. Common sense indicated that a hallucination could not be so steadfastly maintained for a period of three weeks with such consistency and with so much faith and confidence in the reality of the Blessed Virgin's appearance under a barrage of mockery. Medical observers testified that nothing in the manner of her recitation of the Rosary during these weeks indicated a state of exaltation. Even at the very first appearance of the Virgin the thought of apparitions was far from mind as Mariette kept impatiently peering out the window for young Julien's return.

Saturday evening, February 11, brought no suspicion to Mariette that it was to be different from each day of the preceding three weeks as she swung her father's coat over her head, took her place near the bottom of the doorsteps, and began her normal Rosary. Six people were present, among them her father. After the Rosary was finished Mariette rose as though to go indoors, but after a moment decided to continue the prayer standing. Beco himself went into the house. The first four decades went without incident, but suddenly at the fifth Mariette dropped to her knees and all was still. Then the Rosary recommenced in a more expressive and clearer manner. When she again rose and started for the entrance to the front yard, one of the observers, a visiting parish priest, Father Marcas, was struck by the child's beautiful calm and serenity of expression, so clear in the moon's light. His question, "Where are you going, my child?" seemed unheard by Mariette as she passed him on the path leading to the road. Once on the road, she turned toward the spring, making the same genuflections as several weeks before, and continuing the recitation of Aves. At the water source she knelt facing the slight incline of the bank on which Our Lady stood; she leaned forward and plunged her hand into the stream and blessed herself with the cross on the rosary. She remained immobile for several minutes listening intently to Our Lady with a very clear and alert expression. One of the four nurses present noted this especially closely when she took Mariette's pulse and found it to be normal. Mariette's only words were those which concluded the vision: "Thank you, thank you." Quickly she got to her feet, hid with her right arm the tears which now welled up, and headed directly home without the least attention to those about her.

The witnesses followed, crowding into the tiny kitchen. Mariette could do nothing but sob as she rested her head on the kitchen table. The decision to stop pressing their questions and to leave roused Mariette to the plea, "Oh no, wait a little." She sought a private talk with her father in the next room, and through the half-open door Mariette could be heard repeating the words of Our Lady, *"Je viens soulager la souffrance."* She could not understand the French words and asked her father to translate them into Walloon, the French dialect employed in this section of Belgium. Learning that Our Lady said, "I come to relieve suffering," she not only answered all the questions of the witnesses but accompanied them that very night to the parish rectory for an interrogation session with Father Jamin.

Among other things, Father Jamin discovered that the Blessed Virgin arrived and departed as usual through the pines, gradually becoming larger and smaller; that she was dressed as usual; that she glided toward the spring as on the second and third visits; that she closed the interview with a gracious *"au revoir"*; and that the whole apparition lasted only ten minutes.

The next morning would bring the Feast of Our Lady of Lourdes, the seventy-fifth anniversary of Bernadette's visit from heaven. Evidently prompted by Father Marcas, Mariette asked Father Jamin to give her First Holy Communion the next morning. A short, spirited exchange ensued in which Mariette met the priest's objections point by point and in which he finally consented to advance her Communion date. Thus February 12, 1933, Mariette, who only the day before had seen the Blessed Virgin, Heaven's Queen, received in her heart the Treasure of Heaven, Jesus. She had gone from Mary to Jesus.

On February 13 and 14, Mariette recited only two Rosaries during her vigil; the weather was foul and there was no vision.

On February 15, Father Jamin's housekeeper, a local farm woman, and a visiting lady from Liége were present at 7:00 P.M. in the Beco front yard. In addition to these three, Mrs. Beco put in an appearance for the first time, accompanying Mariette, who wore a white beret and a short raincoat. The first Rosary started and was concluded with the witnesses kneeling behind Mariette on the path. At the second decade of the Rosary she stopped. Looking directly at the Virgin of the Poor, who was now in their midst, Mariette announced to the visitor, "Blessed Virgin, the chaplain told me to ask you for a sign." The silence lasted three minutes, and then Mariette continued the second Rosary in a voice that was not sure, forgetting to count the Aves correctly, and trailing off into sobs and tears at the end. A flood of silent tears poured out as the bystanders observed the child prostrate, her face to the earth. Mrs. Beco tried her best to lift the child from the ground, but it took the added strength of another lady to do it. "Why are you crying?" she asked.

Between sobs Mariette admitted, "Because she has gone."

"You have seen her then? Did she answer your question?"

"Yes."

"What did she say?"

" 'Believe in me, I will believe in you. Pray much. *Au revoir.*' "

Every vision was now a mixture of joy and sorrow. The assurance that Our Lady would return never came. No sign would be given— only, "Believe in me." And during this, the sixth apparition, a secret was confided to the child which she could not tell "even to Mamma or Papa." It is useless speculation to discuss whether it was something joyful or sorrowful, something personal or social. Mariette would not give even the slightest indication: "You can kill me just like you do the rabbits, even then I would not tell it!" There was no trip to the spring this time, but the other details of the previous apparitions remained.

Mariette always appeared promptly at seven o'clock so that she would not miss any opportunity of meeting with Our Lady. Thus, as usual, on Monday evening, the twentieth of February, despite the bitter cold, she started the first Rosary on her knees. As the second Rosary began, she joined the other eight witnesses and stood; however, at the end she knelt down abruptly and held her hands out slightly in the direction of the Virgin's usual location; her voice heightened and became more expressive and her prayers became more rapid. After a few moments Mariette rose and started the trip of some 325 feet to the stream reserved by Our Lady for all nations. She fell to her knees three times on the road, as each time Our Lady stopped gliding ahead. Finally, kneeling as beside the ditch in the snow, she prayed a decade, all the while keeping her eyes on the motherly smile of Our Lady. The silence customary when the Blessed Virgin communed with Mariette was followed by Mariette's tears, which she tried to hide with her hands.

Our Lady's grave, unsmiling demeanor this time underlined the essential message of all modern apparitions of Our Lady as she spoke, "My dear child, pray much." Before Mary disappeared she parted with *"au revoir."* When Mr. Beco looked in on Mariette at ten-thirty that evening, he found her beside the bed fingering her beads. Already Our Lady's plea had found one heart—"Pray much."

Though the Lady did not appear from February 20 to March 2, an interval comparable to the January 20—February 11 break, Mariette remained faithful to her seven o'clock vigil every evening. The wintry blasts had gone, but now torrential downpours, some lasting more than three hours, were not unusual. When Mariette ventured forth on the second of March, it was pouring. She was partially protected by an old sack, and over her head she wore a shawl. One of the five ladies who braved the storm held an umbrella over her, as she knelt in the mud. After two Rosaries had been said under such miserable conditions, the rain stopped and the skies cleared, revealing the full brilliancy of the stars and moon. Toward the third decade of the third Rosary the onlookers could tell from the way Mariette opened her arms in welcome and rose and stepped forward that she who called herself the Virgin of the Poor had arrived. Mariette fell back to her knees after the unexpected step forward, and the pace of her Rosary quickened on a higher pitch. Ten more Aves followed before the silent period of listening to Mary began.

All that the ladies heard was a distinct "Yes, yes," one rapidly following the other. This Mariette said in response to the magnificent closing words of the Lady—who today was most serious and even sorrowful in appearance—"I am the Mother of the Savior, Mother of God. Pray much." Then there was the silence of a Mariette ravished by the sight of Mary the Mother of Jesus. As a little of the magnificence of the vision crept into Mariette's heart, her personal dedication to the demand of the Mother of the Savior, Mother of God came "Yes, yes."

As at the fourth apparition the Blessed Virgin stretched forth her hands and blessed Mariette. There were to be no more visits, no more intervals; the Daughter of the Father, Mother of the Son, and the Spouse of the Holy Spirit took leave of the poorest child in the forgotten Belgian village with the final and gracious, "Adieu—till we meet in God," as she glided over the pine trees to come again only in the workings of grace and health for which Banneux is becoming famous.

Continued prayer was impossible, for the child was bowed to the earth in incontrollable sobs.

The father was called from the house, and, cradling Mariette in his arms, he carried her in and laid her on a bed in the rear room. "The Blessed Virgin shall come no more; she said 'Adieu,' " was Mariette's explanation of what appeared to be a complete breakdown. But within a matter of minutes she again was normal, responding to all questions. The apparition had lasted but five minutes, and, like the fourth in the first series, it was the shortest of the second group. Outside the rain again picked up the tempo of externals at Banneux as it monotonously hit the roof of the Beco home.

At Banneux there was no popular piety, only thirty people were present for the best attended apparition, and hardly anyone witnessed more than half of them. Fatima, Lourdes, and Beauraing had their thousands even at the start. Banneux was plain and poor, for the Virgin who called herself the Virgin of the Poor. The inner message of Banneux, contained in the explicit graciousness of the Queen of Heaven, who identified herself with the poor and who appeared as a smiling mother beckoning to her children, is revolutionary.

It is the sense of the message of Banneux which demands our full attention. The events in themselves are the external signs which lead us to the core. Stripped of its quaint particularities, Banneux has the vigorous simplicity of the gospel, with a universal import. That the Blessed Mother should appear in one of the world's smaller countries, Belgium, then announce that she is the special patroness of those universal people, the poor; that a spring is reserved for all nations; and that she is the Mother of the Savior, Mother of God, woudl all seem completely baffling if it were not inserted in the context of traditional Catholic dogma and the needs of our day. Mary, the Mother of Jesus, at Banneux asserts anew, with the force reminiscent of her chant of social revolution, the Magnificat, that hers is a vital role in the Church, especially in the recapture of all society to her Son.

No one can go to Banneux with his booklet of devotions and come away with just a few Novenas finished. That could be but a sickness of individualism, sentimental piety, and egocentric religion. To "place your hands in the water" sparkling from Banneux, to realize sincerely a child-like dependence on Mary, the Mother of Jesus and our Mother, is to know that Mary is more than the greatest of saints, worthy of special veneration. The Marian fountains of Banneux and Lourdes are outward signs of that great reality of Catholic dogma: Christ, the Living Water, has always and will always come to us through Mary.

While the God-Man, Jesus Christ, is our unique mediator before God the Father, the plan of Divine Wisdom has ordained that from the very first moment Christ was present in the world, it was through Mary. Christ alone is the God-chosen cause of the infinite merits which are the price of our redemption, but it is Mary who prepared the sacrificial offering and through her union of will with Christ shared most intimately in the passion and its merits. For us, devotion to Mary leads to devotion to Christ. In this sense, she comes before Christ, preparing us to receive His grace and then nurturing in us that same divine life that she bore within her body at Nazareth.

Mary is the "Virgin of the Poor" because she is always trying to help us out of the poverty of sin, the cramped quarters of self-love, the dingy desolation of sensuality. Because she has the destiny of humanity so intensely at heart, she came to Banneux to remind us again that in God's plan she is the essential link with our Head, Jesus, but that as much as she is willing and can help us, she needs our co-operation.

Through Mary to Jesus is the concise theological statement of Banneux. And it is but the simple device for the great tradition of the Mediation of the Blessed Virgin. Each of the gestures and words of Banneux falls into a complete pattern, which speaks to us only of the loving attentive Mother.

So important is the revelation of Banneux that the visionary Mariette Beco has become completely eclipsed. As the five children of Beauraing, she also is married and has a family, and relentlessly resists all publicity with her fierce natural stubbornness.

Beyond this fragmentary information, the Banneux authorities do not encourage us. Her latest published photos are those of the period immediately following the apparitions. Mariette was the instrument of Our Lady, not the attraction.

That such an apparition should take place in the Belgian province of Liége is not too surprising. On the very day that the Virgin was first appearing to Mariette and beckoning her to come to the spring, symbolic of Christ, the new bishop of the diocese, Louis Joseph Kerkhofs was surrounded by his people in the cathedral basilica of St. Martin in Liége to consecrate the new year to Mary under the title of *The Mother of All.* The province of Liége was prepared for the smiles of the Virgin of the Poor, the Mother of the Savior, Mother of God, Mediatrix of all graces for men. Belgium, too, is the first country to have obtained from the Holy See the special liturgical celebration of the feast of Mary, Mediatrix of All Graces.

While few were at first attracted to Banneux and even fewer of these were convinced of the supernatural character of Mariette Beco's story, the cult to the Virgin of the Poor grew steadily until on the Feast of the Immaculate Heart of Mary, 1949, Bishop Kerkhofs announced the definitive approval of the reality and message of Banneux's 1933 apparitions. His action was not hasty. In March of 1942 a pastoral letter to his diocese announced that late in 1941 the case of Banneux, which had been submitted to the Vatican in 1937—after extensive preliminary evidence had been assembled and evaluated by a Belgian commission during the years

1935–37—had received clearance in Rome. All further investigations and approvals were now fully in the authority of the bishop of Liége. May of 1942 saw the solemn and official inauguration and approval of the cult of the Virgin of the Poor, which had for years developed privately, with the toleration of the prudent and reserved Belgian hierarchy, through the devotion of countless pilgrims. The year 1947 had seen the reiteration of the preliminary approbation.

In the silver jubilee year of 1958, Bishop Kerkhofs' pastoral letter to his diocese and all pilgrims of the Virgin of the Poor pointed the direction of all future work for Banneux: "What is now important is not again the recognition of the *facts* of Banneux, but the understanding and spreading of the *message* of the Virgin of the Poor."

Aside from such primary evidence of the reality of the apparition as the thorough documentation of the whole case from the first apparition; the ten years of painstaking studies by René Rutten, S.J.; the immediate testing and final verification by medical and ecclesiastical authorities as to the absence of any possible natural explanation for the phenomenon; the balanced Marian theology involved; the *fruits* of Banneux present the conclusive arguments.

Thus Bishop Kerkhofs, in his work, *Notre-Dame de Banneux* (studies and documents), lists twenty miraculous cures which took place between May 21, 1933, and 1938. These are only the cases which met the rigid tests of medical records.

But the great work of Our Lady at Banneux is that of extending her maternal embrace to the life of grace in each member of the mystical body of which she is the Mother. The spiritual work of Banneux necessarily cannot be measured in an ordinary way. The well over 500,000 pilgrims who now yearly travel in Mariette's footsteps keep a staff of priests in the confessionals continually during the influx of the summer. The over two million members of the International Union of Prayers join with that Rosary, which has been recited continually at Banneux each evening at seven o'clock since the Virgin first appeared, to pray for the poor, the suffering, and peace among all nations. Works of charity such as the Home of the Vierge des Pauvres for children; the nine religious orders who teach, pray, serve on Banneux's plain; the 250-bed hospital, where three-day retreats are held for the sick; the five national centers of information on and devotion to the Virgin of the Poor; the 300 chapels, the over 3000 monuments and shrines, and 25 churches throughout the world dedicated to the Virgin of the Poor are all eloquent testimony to the spirituality of Banneux.

From the fact that the first stone was laid for the charming open-air chapel (which became a model for many others throughout the world) in March of 1933 on the site of the first apparition, and that the first authenticated miracle transpired May 21, 1933, it was evident Our Lady really meant to establish her reign at Banneux.

The two small, open chapels, one next to the Beco home, the other over the spot where Our Lady appeared at the spring, are the focal points of the pilgrim. Only after twenty-five years was the single pump spring capped and its source directed into multiple outlets in a wall extending along both sides of the spring.

The recently constructed enclosure of St. Joseph with its sacristy, extra altars and confessionals; the Curé of Ars shelter for priests serving the Banneux pilgrims; the Hospitalité for the sick—all are planned unobtrusively to keep everything under the mastery of rustic simplicity. Even the vast basilica to Our Lady, Queen of Nations, so badly needed because of the rainy weather, will blend with that gracious, unaffected dignity keynoted by the Virgin herself as she bent over Mariette.

That the unrolling, flat landscape of a Belgian hamlet, Banneux-Notre-Dame, drew down to its dull farmlands the Mother of Jesus for eight apparitions in 1933, and that she chose such a poor and obscure spot is not a surprise to her children. She is most at home in places like Nazareth and Bethlehem. That she should come to us at all cannot astound the believer who knows that her one vital interest is the extension of the life of Christ in us so that we may be more perfectly her children. Banneux is a new occasion for thankfulness to Almighty God that He has granted us the Queen of Heaven as the Motherly Mediatrix of His grace.

BIOGRAPHICAL
SKETCHES OF
THE CONTRIBUTORS

JOHN J. DELANEY

A native New Yorker, John Delaney has always been fascinated with books, which are his livelihood, lifework, and chief hobby. He has been connected with some aspect of the book business since his high school days and is now editor of the famous Doubleday *Image Books*. In addition, he selects the books of the Catholic Family Book Club and Catholic Youth Book Club, and is a senior editor in charge of original Catholic publications at Doubleday & Company, Inc., in New York. He has lectured in various parts of the United States, has appeared on national television and radio programs, and has had articles published in leading Catholic magazines. He is also originator and general editor of the *Catholic Viewpoint Series*. In 1958 he was the recipient of the Catholic Press Association—Catholic Digest Award for "distinguished service to Christian journalism and publishing."

REV. JOSEPH I. DIRVIN, C.M.

A native of Germantown, Pennsylvania, Fr. Dirvin is a graduate of St. Joseph's College in Princeton and was ordained as a Vincentian priest in 1943. He served for eleven years as assistant to Rev. Joseph A. Skelly,

C.M., at The Central Association of the Miraculous Medal in Germantown and as Associate Editor of *The Miraculous Medal* magazine, and in recent years has taught at St. John's University in New York where he is presently Dean of Men. He has written several pamphlets, a one-act play, and *St. Catherine Labouré of the Miraculous Medal*, which is regarded as the definitive biography of St. Catherine Labouré.

ETHEL COOK ELIOT

Ever since early childhood Ethel Cook Eliot had the desire to write. The daughter of a Congregationalist minister in North Gage, New York, she was raised in Pittsfield, Massachusetts, and when, in her senior high school year, *Harper's Monthly* published a poem by her, she knew she had found her career in life. She engaged in editorial work on several New York magazines, wrote special magazine articles, and began freelance writing. She married Samuel Atkins Eliot, Jr., the grandson of the famous Harvard president, and became a resident of Northampton, Massachusetts, where she still lives, when he became professor of drama at Smith College in 1918. She has written more than a dozen books, fairy tales, juveniles and novels, and *Roses for Mexico*, of which Joseph Henry Jackson, the distinguished critic of the San Francisco *Monitor*, said: "It is likely, I think, that her re-telling of the ancient legend will become the classic one in English."

MSGR. JOHN S. KENNEDY

Msgr. John S. Kennedy, widely regarded as one of the outstanding Catholic literary critics in the United States, is a native New Englander and a priest of the Hartford archdiocese where he was raised and educated. His weekly book column in *The Catholic Transcript*, "Balancing the Books," was widely syndicated and is regarded by hundreds of thousands of readers as the outstanding review column in the United States; his column of general observations, "The Sifting Floor," was one of the most popular features of the *Transcript* until press of work caused him to discontinue it in 1958. He has lectured all over the United States, has appeared on national radio and television programs, and has had articles published in many Catholic magazines. He was made a Domestic Prelate by Pope Pius XII in 1955, and appointed Editor of the *Transcript* in 1954. He has written three books, *Pleased to Meet You, The Common Cross,* and *Light on the Mountain,* the story of La Salette, which in 1953 received the Marian Library Medal as the best book on Our Lady published in that year.

FRANCES PARKINSON KEYES

Frances Parkinson Keyes is one of the most popular authors of our times. Many of her novels are high on the all-time, best-seller lists, and each of her new books is eagerly awaited by millions of readers anxious to savor the joys of a new Keyes novel. She was born at the University of Virginia, where her father, a Bostonian, was head of the Greek Department; but he died when she was only two years old, and her mother's marriage to another Bostonian took her back to New England, where she grew up and received her education, except for two years spent in Europe, a decade apart. At the age of eighteen she married Henry Wilder Keyes, who later became Governor of New Hampshire and served three terms from that state in the United States Senate, retiring just before his death. She has traveled all over the world and become known as one of Washington's most gracious hostesses, a reputation she continues to enjoy in New Orleans, which she now uses as a writing center during the winter, and in New Hampshire, which is still her legal residence. Her writing career began with her first novel, *The Old Gray Homestead,* an article in *Atlantic Monthly,* entitled "The Satisfied Reflections of a Semi-Bostonian," and a series of articles, "Letters from a Senator's Wife," in *Good Housekeeping* which were tremendously popular. Since then a succession of books, among them *Senator Marlowe's Daughter, Joy Street, The Royal Box,* and *Blue Camellia,* have made publishing history. In 1936 she was sent to Lisieux to write a life of the Little Ste. Thérèse, and this first excursion into hagiography was so successful that it led to a series of books on religious subjects, most recent of which are a biography of St. Anne and *Land of Stones and Saints,* for which latter the Spanish government bestowed on her the Order of Isabella the Catholic. She has also been awarded the Siena Medal as "outstanding Catholic woman of the year" in the United States and the Médaille Reconnaissance Française in recognition of her work toward the restoration of the Benedictine Abbaye in Lisieux, where Ste. Thérèse went to school and made her First Communion. Mrs. Keyes has spent considerable time in Lourdes, has written widely on the miraculous happenings there (*The Sublime Shepherdess,* revised and reissued as *Bernadette of Lourdes* in 1953, *Guadalupe to Lourdes,* articles on Bernadette, "My Favorite Saint" in *The Sign* and "The Lesson of Lourdes" in *America*), and is considered one of the outstanding American authorities on this famous apparition.

MSGR. WILLIAM C. McGRATH

A native of Newfoundland, Msgr. McGrath was ordained in 1921 and after a year at the cathedral at St. John's joined the Scarboro Foreign Mission Society in Toronto. He was editor of the Society's monthly magazine *China* for ten years, went to China in 1931, was appointed Prefect Apostolic of the Canadian mission at Lishui, Chekiang, in 1932, and returned to Canada in 1939 and was Vicar General of the Society until 1942. Since October of 1947 he has been Director of the Pilgrim Virgin Tour of the United States. In that capacity he has covered more than half a million miles on his various tours and has told some ten million people the story of the awesome events at Fatima in 1917 and the message for the world given there to the three shepherd children by Our Lady. Unquestionably, he is in the fore of those who have labored so successfully to make Our Lady of Fatima known to her numerous followers. He has written *The Dragon at Close Range*, an intimate close-up of mission life in China, and *Fatima or World Suicide*, in which he discusses the alternatives facing America and the world if they reject Our Lady's message at Fatima.

ROBERT M. MALOY, S.M.

Brother Robert Maloy is a native of Cleveland and a graduate of the University of Dayton. He joined the Society of Mary (Marianists) in 1952 and is now librarian of the University of Dayton's Marian Library which has one of the world's greatest collections of books, manuscripts, and other material on Our Lady. He is also editor of the Marian Library *Newsletter* and managing editor of the *Marianist*.

MARY PURCELL

Mary Purcell was born in the little village of Carrigeen, Mooncoin, County Kilkenny, a few miles from the Atlantic coast of Ireland. The daughter of schoolteachers, she has taught in Irish schools since 1928, and for the past several years has been teaching cerebral palsied children. She is assistant editor of the Irish edition of *Messenger of the Sacred Heart* and has had several articles on shrines and saints published in American Catholic magazines. She attracted favorable literary attention with the publication of a life of St. Joan of Arc, *The Halo on the Sword*, in 1950. Since that time she has written *Don Francisco: The Story of St. Francis Xavier*, *Matt Talbot and His Times*, and *The First Jesuit: St.*

Ignatius Loyola, which has been called by many authorities the best biography of the founder of the Jesuits. She has traveled all over Europe, has written many articles on the lives of various saints, shrines, and Catholic history, and is considered one of the outstanding Catholic writers of present-day Ireland.

DON SHARKEY

Since his high school days in Middleton, Ohio, where he was born, Don Sharkey has been writing newspaper pieces, magazine articles, pamphlets, and books. After his graduation from the University of Dayton in 1934, he worked for a publishing company, was editor of the *Young Catholic Messenger* for ten years, and resigned in 1949 to devote himself exclusively to writing. He has had articles published in practically every Catholic periodical in the country and since 1951 has been writing a series of history texts for elementary schools. His research for *After Bernadette, The Story of Modern Lourdes* in 1945 raised his interest in Our Lady to a fervent pitch. Since then he has worked ceaselessly and untiringly to spread devotion to Mary in articles, talks and books, and his column, "This Is Your Mother," which appeared in *The Ave Maria* and was the outstanding Marian column in the United States. Among his books are *White Smoke over the Vatican, The Woman Shall Conquer*, and he is co-author of *Our Lady of Beauraing*, which received the 1957 Marian Library Medal as the outstanding book on Our Lady.

Printed in the United States
by Baker & Taylor Publisher Services